DARE, DREAM, DO

Praise for the book

'This is the story of Anandiben, but also the story of India's democracy. The potential of democracy to empower all citizens and encourage women to take up leadership roles is best exemplified by your remarkable career. That you have served the nation with full commitment while also taking care of the family during your formative years speaks volumes about nari shakti… I look forward to getting more acquainted with your personal journey and your values that shaped your struggles. Your recollections about people who influenced your choices early on and about your close association with leaders, including Prime Minister Narendra Modi, will provide rich material for historians. More importantly, *Dare, Dream, Do* will inspire young women to dedicate themselves, like you have, to the task of nation-building.'

—Ram Nath Kovind, former President of India

'From being a gallantry award winner to being a teacher, from becoming the first woman Chief Minister of Gujarat to being appointed the Governor of Uttar Pradesh, Smt. Anandiben Patel had an inspiring and remarkable life journey. I am confident her life story will further motivate younger generations, especially public representatives, to serve the country and our people to the best of their abilities.'

—M. Venkaiah Naidu, former Vice President of India

'The life story of Smt. Anandiben Patel ji is inspiring and remarkable. It is a saga of the struggles and achievements as well as the experiences and exposures of an eminent personality. Born into a family in rural Gujarat, she grew up in an environment where education was given prime importance. Her life-long commitment for education started as a dedicated student. Her association with education continued as she initiated her career as a teacher and then principal. As education minister of Gujarat, Smt. Patel initiated a number of steps to promote education. Hon'ble Governor's dedication for education is manifested in her decisions and actions as chancellor of state universities of Uttar Pradesh. Brave, determined and dedicated, Smt. Anandiben Patel ji holds the rare distinction of being Gujarat's first woman chief minister. As a minister of the government of Gujarat, she made significant contributions. She discharged her duties as MLA and Member of Parliament with great zeal. Smt. Anandiben Patel ji has devoted her life for the betterment of the weaker sections, especially women. I hope that this book will provide an insight into how we all can become true leaders with a kind heart.'

—Yogi Adityanath, Chief Minister of Uttar Pradesh

'The story of a girl, brought up in a humble farmer family in a small village named Kharod, who opens her wings braving all odds to become the first woman chief minister of one of the most prosperous states of India to the governor of Uttar Pradesh has been inspirational and worth telling… I wish the biography of the "Veerbala of Mehsana" will be instrumental in infusing new courage and hope in the readers…'

—Bhupendra Patel, Chief Minister of Gujarat

'A gripping biography of a leader and administrator, who led from the front and left an indelible mark. A must-read book for anyone who wants to rise from the roots in service of society.'

—Uday Mahurkar, Information Commissioner,
Government of India

'It was a pleasure working with Anandiben, as secretary of the department, during her first tenure as education minister. She initiated many innovative schemes like appointment of Vidya Sahayaks, construction of prefab classrooms, a transparent system of teachers' transfers, bar coding of board answer sheets and many others.'

—Sudhir Mankad, former Chief Secretary, Government of Gujarat

'Our Hon'ble Chancellor Smt. Anandiben Patel is an epitome of leadership, which entails courage and empathy that imbues the charismatic personality of a successful politician, devoted to upholding egalitarian values in society. The political journey presents her dauntless and impeccable career, exhibiting her unflinching belief in service to society. In the last three years, she has devotedly worked for higher education and advancing the quality of education in the state of Uttar Pradesh. She has played a path-breaking role in the recruitment process, which yields in quality teachers in the universities and her contribution to the implementation of NEP 2020 and NAAC is exemplary. Also, she has made an extraordinary effort in terms of social responsibility as people drew inspiration from her and adopted more than 1,25,000 TB patients and 2,500 anganwadis.'

—Dr Vinay Pathak, Vice Chancellor,
Chhtrapati Shahu Ji Maharaj University, Kanpur

'Smt. Anandiben Patel ji, with the strength of her personality, the force which propelled the destiny of a state and its progeny, has conquered the obstacles with realistic courage and envisioned a change in the future of the country through education. This extraordinary towering personality, whose aura spreads beyond imagination, has created new standards as a custodian of democracy as governor of the largest state of India, Uttar Pradesh. She is the voice for equality, determination and dignity, and has pioneered the era of transformation in education, thus creating a silent revolution—accomplished purely by her persona. She has rewritten the syntax for leadership, i.e. to inspire and lead the people, so that they inclusively act in making a nation.'

—Dr S.C. Sharma, Director, NAAC, Bangalore

'This is a fascinating and inspirational journey of an educationist, athlete, a courageous woman who received the president's gallantry award, fighting for bird flu victims and upliftment of women and downtrodden, who despite her personal and professional struggles reached the highest office as first woman chief minister of Gujrat and governor to several states of India.'

—Dr Radha Krishan Dhiman, Director, Sanjay Gandhi Postgraduate Institute of Medical Sciences, Lucknow

'...Having carved a path for herself through her struggle and her courage, Anandiben Patel ji's life is an example for women of how womankind is the embodiment of power. Women's issues are not just a topic of debate and discussion for her. I have seen her staunchly support women's causes on many occasions...'

—Malini Awasthi, Padma Shri folk singer

'Hon'ble Anandiben Patelji's life, career and inspiring example are a true testament to her incredible love and dedication to the nation. Her service is her meditation in action and her prayer and puja in action. Through her dedicated service, she transforms the most mundane situations into great possibility and potential for positive change. May her story and her life continue to inspire young leaders across the nation and across the world to be the change they want to see in the world and to utilize power and privilege for the greater good and as powerful tools of social transformation.'

—Pujya Swami Chidanand Saraswatiji, President, Parmarth Niketan, Rishikesh

DARE, DREAM, DO

The Extraordinary Life of
Anandiben Patel

As told to **ANURAG GARG**

RUPA

First published by
Rupa Publications India Pvt. Ltd 2022
7/16, Ansari Road, Daryaganj
New Delhi 110002

Sales Centres:

Allahabad Bengaluru Chennai
Hyderabad Jaipur Kathmandu
Kolkata Mumbai

P-ISBN: 978-93-5520-554-4
E-ISBN: 978-93-5520-556-8

First impression 2022

10 9 8 7 6 5 4 3 2 1

Printed in India

Contents

From the Desk of the President of India

It gives me immense pleasure to know that Smt. Anandiben Patel is sharing her unusual life history in the form of a book titled *Dare, Dream, Do*.

The teacher turned politician, Smt. Patel made history when she took charge as Gujarat's first woman chief minister. She is a socially inclined politician and an able administrator. In her long and distinguished public career, she touched many lives in innumerable ways—as a school teacher, social worker, parliamentarian, administrator, as chief minister of the state of Gujarat and governor of Madhya Pradesh, Chhattisgarh and currently Uttar Pradesh. The saga of her struggle and strength of character will inspire the women of our country to take leadership role in every sphere of life.

I extend my warm greetings and felicitations to all those associated with this book and send my best wishes for the success of the publication.

Droupadi Murmu
President of India

Reflections

It is heartening to gather that a senior politician and high constitutional functionary Smt. Anandiben Patel has chosen to pen her autobiography. It expresses, in a significant manner, her experiences in the political, societal and constitutional ecosystem. The autobiography is bound to be anecdotal and informative apart from being an inspiration for many. This is bound to be dotted by instances and incidents known and otherwise, during her exemplary career in multifaceted areas.

Her journey from a humble school teacher to the high offices of chief minister and governor exemplifies her deep commitment, understanding and appreciation of the ground reality. The reminiscences in her autobiography of all these years would certainly reflect her sincere commitments to bring about changes in the lives of people, particularly her gender. I have enormously benefitted out of interactions with her on several occasions and each one has left an indelible impression on my mind.

An autobiography is indeed a challenge and I am sure Smt. Anandiben Patel has done full justice to it.

Jagdeep Dhankhar
Vice President of India

Foreword

I am pleased to learn about the publication of the autobiography of Smt Anandiben Patel Ji. The endeavour to chart the voyage of her life will make for compelling reading.

Blessed with a humble disposition, Anandiben has made a remarkable contribution during her public life spanning over decades. Be it as an educator, Karyakarta, minister and chief minister of Gujarat, or during her tenure as governor, her steadfast efforts towards serving the nation and people have been noteworthy.

As a youngster, Anandiben was among very few girls who went to school at a time when education of girls was not considered as a priority by many. She was a bright student and a fine athlete. Fearless and compassionate, she was conferred the President's bravery award for saving two girls from drowning in Sardar Sarovar reservoir.

I am sure that this autobiography will bring to light several other lesser-known facets of her life. May she continue to work for larger good in the years to come.

May the book inspire youngsters to integrate their aspirations and efforts with our national goals. Best wishes for all success of the publication.

Narendra Modi
Prime Minister of India

Full Circle

Strength does not come from physical capacity.
It comes from an indomitable will.

—Mahatma Gandhi

29 July 2019
Raj Bhavan, Lucknow, Uttar Pradesh

It was a historic and promising day for Uttar Pradesh (UP)—one of the most political states in India. With roughly 200 million inhabitants, it is the most populous state in the country and the most populous country subdivision in the world. Created on 1 April 1937 as the United Provinces of Agra and Oudh (also Avadh) during British rule, the state was renamed Uttar Pradesh in 1950. It is divided into 18 divisions and 75 districts, with Lucknow as its capital.

The Raj Bhavan estate in Lucknow is a 200-year-old historical building designed by Frenchman Major-General Claude Martin, who was also made the chief architect in Nawab Asaf-ud-Daula's darbar. Raj Bhavan used to be called Kothi Hayat Baksh; the term 'Hayat Baksh' means 'life-giving'.

The two-storeyed palatial building, situated on the eastern side of the city, is surrounded by lush greenery. For the oath-taking ceremony, the courtyard, constructed in the traditional Indian architectural style, was decorated to welcome the 25th governor of the state. The Iron Lady of Gujarat was going to be sworn in at Raj Bhavan. Anandiben Patel, the first woman chief minister of Gujarat (2014–16), acquired this title due to her dedicated work over several decades in the rural areas of Gujarat. She was the one who made the state vibrant, along with India's present prime minister, Narendra Modi. Her memories of working with Modi find mention in later parts of this book.

Raj Bhavan was abuzz with activity on the day of the oath-taking ceremony. Its high-roofed verandahs were covered with marigold garlands. The arches of the *dewankhana* were decorated with floral motifs and beautifully painted golden. Commandos and police officials were lined up at Mahatma Gandhi Marg. Lucknow's Mall Avenue locality was spruced up from top to bottom. Raj Bhavan looked truly enchanting with its everlasting splendour of beautifully designed curly railings, lush greenery, tall trees, beautiful gardens, fountains and lighting.

During British rule, Raj Bhavan was Major-General Claude Martin's residence and had all the arrangements for his security guards and armoury. On 18 March 1857, our freedom fighters attacked this building, then the headquarters of the British Army. Even before India gained independence, Kothi Hayat Baksh was declared as the official residence of the governor of the United Provinces of Agra and Avadh. Raj Bhavan was given its final present shape during that time. The British governors resided here prior to Independence, and afterwards it became the official residence of the Indian governors. This building acquired its name after Independence. The first governor of UP, Sarojini Naidu, lived here until April 1948.

At 10.20 a.m., in honour of the future governor, the army band, consisting of pipes, drums, buglers and trumpeters, welcomed Anandiben Patel at Chaudhary Charan Singh Airport (formerly Amausi Airport) in Lucknow. Dressed in a traditional emerald green silk saree, Anandiben came into view, deboarding from an Indian government aircraft. On her arrival at the runway, the commandos leaped from their black Scorpios and sprinted towards the aircraft while police officials in khaki stood on high alert, ready to provide cover.

At the airport, Chief Minister Yogi Adityanath, the serving chief minister of UP currently in his second term, and his convoy consisting of bulletproof SUVs, jammers and an ambulance, also arrived to greet the new governor. Anandiben Patel walked out on the red carpet with her aide-de-camp (ADC) officer and security in charge. The police officials lined up on one side of the red carpet and presented the guard of honour to receive the governor as the head of the state, followed by a warm welcome from the Chief Minister. Anandiben Patel saluted the officials and marched towards Raj Bhavan with her convoy.

Chief Justice Govind Mathur, who administered the oath, also arrived at Raj Bhavan. The guests gathered at the Gandhi Sabhagar, an auditorium in the main building of Raj Bhavan. During British rule, it was used as a ballroom and, later came to be known as the Durbar Hall. It had wooden flooring with springs attached within that made the floor bouncy. After Independence, it was converted into an auditorium with a stage where various events, such as seminars, cultural programmes and something as important as the oath-taking ceremony of the governor, are organized. Deputy Chief Minister Keshav Prasad Maurya, Dr Dinesh Sharma and outgoing governor, Ram Naik, were also present at the ceremony.

A fountain depicting the seal of the state government adorns Raj Bhavan's main entrance. Statues depicting the holy rivers of Ganga, Yamuna and Saraswati as well as a pair of leaping fish and a marble umbrella add to the beauty of the garden. The magnificent building holds countless historical memories deep in its heart. Endowed with regal dignity, it is a beautiful example of Indo-European architecture. The lush green lawns and majestic white building make it an eye-catching structure. The hall is surrounded by a corridor, which is decorated with flowers and the portraits of former governors of the United Province (before Independence) and Uttar Pradesh (after Independence). The carvings on the walls and ceiling of this auditorium are a wonderful specimen of ancient art.

The trumpets blew again, this time much louder. Everyone stood up to greet Anandiben Patel, who had served as governor of Chhattisgarh and Madhya Pradesh prior to being appointed as governor of UP, and the officials and staff members at Raj Bhavan greeted her with bouquets.

The audience remained in attention as the state's second woman governor arrived to take the oath, succeeding Ram Naik. The officers lined up on the stage as Chief Justice Mathur, Ram Naik and

Anandiben settled into their seats on the dais. Ministers and other government officials took their respective seats in the auditorium and the ceremony commenced with the national anthem.

The officer started with a welcome speech, introduced the guests of the day and requested Chief Justice Govind Mathur to take charge of the ceremony, who then invited Anandiben to take the podium for the oath.

Anandiben, 77, stood up and walked towards the dais with the same grace and force of belief that she had in her early political years. In the previous three decades, she had taken oaths on various platforms for different ranks and has been one of the few leaders who have kept the inviolability of power unspoiled. Anandiben's integrity, honour and determination are worth the admiration of her followers.

'I request Smt. Anandiben Patel to repeat the oath after me,' declared the Chief Justice as he read from the file that every governor and person discharging the functions of the governor shall, before entering upon his office, make and subscribe in the presence of the Chief Justice of the high court of the exercising jurisdiction.

Anandiben adjusted her spectacles and repeated after the Chief Justice in her strong and appealing voice:

'In the name of God, I, Anandiben Patel, solemnly affirm that I will faithfully execute the office of Governor (or discharge the functions of the Governor) of Uttar Pradesh and will to the best of my ability, preserve, protect and defend the Constitution and the law and that I will devote myself to the service and well-being of the people of Uttar Pradesh.'

She signed the oath document amidst the clicking of cameras and murmurs as Ram Naik, who had been in office from 2014 to 2019, stood up and congratulated her. As part of the ceremony, Anandiben took over Ram Naik's chair on stage to a huge round of applause and cheering. That day, UP witnessed a big day of transformation as the Iron Lady of Gujarat took on the responsibilities of the governor.

The ceremony concluded with high tea and snacks prepared by Raj Bhavan's staff. Anandiben greeted all the officials and guests, and expressed her gratitude, while everyone present congratulated her. Her dedication and commitment were such that she decided to begin work the same day. Anandiben took a tour of her residence, as carrying out an inspection had become second nature to her ever since she had joined politics on Modi's persuasion in 1987. When she was appointed the president of the Gujarat Mahila Morcha, she would visit villages and see what needed to be done. She always made it a point to spend time learning how the political system works.

'This is such a beautiful garden,' she said as she looked at the different flowers. 'Is it open to the public?'

The officials looked at each other and one of them responded, 'No, madam.'

'Open it for all!' she exclaimed and marched ahead. Anandiben believes that people should have the first right to access government buildings. On her first day itself, she visited the Rajkiya Balgreh (Shishu) orphanage and interacted with the children there. Being a teacher herself, she knew what needed to be done in the field of education. She met children from different schools, discussed the challenges they faced in their studies, and offered them fruit.

'Who is a governor?' an innocent girl child asked Anandiben. The teachers elbowed each other and tried to signal the girl to stop her from asking such questions. Anandiben smiled and caressed her head lovingly, and said, 'A governor is the one who takes care of everyone in the state.'

After meeting the children, Anandiben went back to Raj Bhavan and met all the staff members in the kitchen garden. She asked about their children and family members. 'Who knows how to cook Gujarati food?' Everyone looked at each other. It was clear that they did not have much idea about Gujarati food.

'Don't worry, I will train you,' Anandiben said, laughing, and returned to her room. She is the perfect example of courage and compassion; a true leader who knows how to work with everyone as a family—one unit—and serve the main purpose of her existence: working towards the betterment of humanity.

Over the next few days, Anandiben got busy. Among the several things she did at Raj Bhavan, one of them was visiting the cow sheds and feeding jaggery to the cows. She spent time with the animals and caressed them like she used to when she was a child. There was a huge *charagah* (pasture) for the animals close to the *astabal* (stable) for royal horses on the northwest side of Raj Bhavan. A small group of people lived here to take care of the animals. These people were called the Naldars and it was their duty to keep the horses of the British royal forces fit and ready. The stable also houses cows, hens and goats now to make fresh dairy products available.

Anandiben met Chief Minister Yogi Adityanath and discussed state issues and the work to be done. For her, the priority has always been education, as she believes that the solution to most problems is access to good education. She asked the officials to schedule a visit to nearby anganwadis (childcare centres) and met the women and children there to asses the state of education at the grassroots level. She also invited the children of the anganwadi to Raj Bhavan.

In the same week, Anandiben met the vice chancellors of all the state universities and proposed strengthening the education system. Her in-depth knowledge of the issues and her experience in the education sector was known across the country. People would give the example of her work in education, especially in Gujarat, where she reformed the entire system, which had been neglected for years.

On 15 August 2019, Anandiben hoisted the flag at Raj Bhavan, which was followed by a cultural event. Raksha Bandhan was celebrated with the girls from Prajapita Brhamkumari Ishwariya University. The officials distributed books, pens and other stationery items to underprivileged children. Anandiben tied rakhis to Chief Minister Yogi Adityanath and Deputy Chief Minister Dr Dinesh Sharma.

After the event scheduled for the day, as per her daily routine, she walked 5 kilometres. Her discipline was exemplary. That day, she emerged to walk in the evening and security officials recorded her coordinates.

It was Independence Day, and to her, the day always meant something special and honourable. She removed her slippers and walked barefoot on the grass. As soon as her feet touched the ground, she felt connected to Mother Earth. Her grounded nature and her quest to remain connected with her roots went beyond luxury and power.

As she walked alone in the garden that was covered with tall trees, she heard a squeal and a rumble. The sounds were coming from somewhere above her. She looked up and saw that it was a group of Indian Air Force jets. Spontaneously, she followed the direction of the jets, wishing to run after them like she used to as a child. The smile on her face and the sparkle in her eyes were extremely childlike. She waved at the jets, allowing patriotic feelings, associated with the celebrations of India's Independence Day, to take over.

Her career had come full circle—a life spent among the people, knowing them, helping them and fighting for them.

The Early Years

Happiness is when what you think,
what you say, and what you do are in harmony.

—Mahatma Gandhi

15 August 1947, Mehsana, Gujarat

'Andi, oh Andi!' a bleak voice echoed in the paddy fields of Kharod village, but six-year-old Anandi did not look back as she was busy gazing at the sky. The child kept on running, her *chaniya* (ghaghra of sorts worn mostly in Gujarat) tightly scooped above the knees to avoid falling. Two oiled braids sailed behind her in the wind.

'*Ahi avo* (come here), Andi!' She stopped to look back at her mother, Menaben, standing near the pen where the animals were housed. She then looked up again at the aeroplane, a distant roar in the skies, slowly disappearing. She ran in the direction of the retreating aeroplane. Baa tapped her forehead dismissively and went back.

As Andi streamed through the field, she lost her grip on her chaniya and it got entangled around her legs. She slipped and fell in the mud, hurting her knee in the process. Unperturbed, she stood up and wiped off the mud. When she looked up again, the aeroplane was still visible. Waving at the plane, she whispered, '*Aawjo* (come again).' With a broad smile, a mud-stained chaniya-choli and a bleeding knee, Andi walked back towards her house, head held high.

Anandiben Patel, a spirited young girl, was born on 21 November 1941, when the Indian subcontinent was ruled by the British Crown. Her village, Kharod, was a quiet, semi-rural village with a population of about 5,000 people living peacefully with little ambition or dreams. The Patel house, the only brick structure there, stood amidst the paddy fields.

Anandiben's father, Jethabhai Patel, was one of the most respected people in the village. He worked as a teacher for a few years, but after his brother's sudden demise, he took up farming and served the villagers. He was a short yet strong man who wore khadi, thick spectacles and a Gandhi cap. The cap, named after Mahatma Gandhi, who popularized it during the Indian independence movement, was commonly worn by Indian independence activists.

Jethabhai was a Gandhian and lived by the values of truth, non-violence, harmony and simplicity. He was a highly moral human being who was connected with his roots, which is reflected in Anandiben too. He was one of the headmen who often weighed in on the village panchayat's decisions. He was involved in solving disputes within the village boundaries. Immensely respected in the community, he always stood up for women's rights and the education of the girl child, and was against caste-based discrimination. He was also one of the few farmers who were educated and practised sustainable methods of farming.

Before Independence, Shrimant Maharaja Pratap Singh Rao Gaekwad, belonging to the Gaekwad dynasty of the Marathas, was the ruling maharaja of Baroda (now Vadodara). He had succeeded to the throne upon the death of his grandfather Sayajirao Gaekwad III in 1939. In the jan-sabhas of Maharaja Gaekwad, Jethabhai used to be consulted for his valuable suggestions pertaining to incidents in the village. He also used to help Dalit widows and other women who were not able to get married because of societal discrimination by finding grooms for them. Additionally, he looked after the development of the village.

Jethabhai would often find himself boycotted by society because in helping these widows, he, apparently, violated many societal norms. Sometimes, because of his actions, he was asked to live outside his village. Once he had to live like that for over a year. He had built his house on farmland, and every time he was asked to leave it, the villagers provided no help to him, but he was self-sufficient and managed to take care of himself and his big family all by himself.

These are the values and beliefs that Anandiben inherited from her father. She was his staunchest follower, and has fought to stand for what is right all her life.

Another field that Jethabhai set an example in was agriculture. He would help the villagers by making fertilizers using cow dung and urine, mixed with dry leaves, residue from crops and water. He was one of the few who ideated rainwater harvesting. He also employed innovations like creating water pipelines and diverting them towards the fields. The dearth of technology did not bother Jethabhai—he overcame all challenges that came his way and ran the farms perfectly.

Jethabhai, a farmer by heart, had agricultural land spread over more than 100 acres. The land was an oasis of tranquillity. There was a huge water tank and a tube well made of mud for bathing and the house, located a few kilometres away from the city, was surrounded by mango, citrus and coconut trees.

Following the aeroplane adventure, Anandi entered the house and washed herself. She then went to the kitchen and helped her mother churn fresh butter. It was a cloudy day. Villages in Gujarat had been waiting for the rains. Close to the fields, she could hear her brothers and father ploughing the fields while singing the verses of the Ramayana. She heard,

> 'हो, मंगल भवन अमंगल हारी, द्रवहुसुदसरथ अचर बिहारी।'
> 'May that home of bliss and bane of woe take compassion on me; He who sports in the courtyard of King Dashratha.'

Anandiben fondly remembers how she loved eating fresh butter and bajra roti from the kitchen quietly, without anyone getting to know what she was doing. However, that eventful day in the nation's history was also among the most memorable incidents from her childhood.

'We are free today, we got our freedom,' Anandiben told her toddler sister while eating some butter.

'What is freedom, Anandi?' her father asked. He was back from the fields and stood by the door along with her eldest brother, Keshubhai.

Anandi stood up. She respected her father very much. For her, his words were valuable lessons of life. 'Freedom is… We are free to play, free to eat butter, free to run on the farm,' said Anandi, her eyes filled with innocence.

Her father and brother chuckled at her naiveté. He put his hand on her head and said, 'Yes, Anandi, freedom means that you are free to do anything, but it also comes with responsibility. It gives you a chance and the ability to become something. It gives you a choice to do, say and think as you wish. We need to take care of this freedom. It should not be misused; this freedom is hard-earned and is a result of many years of fight. So be free, but be responsible.'

'How do we become responsible?' she asked in her brittle voice.

'We have to ensure that our freedom makes us progress. We have to take care of everything around us: our farms, our house, our animals, our education, our people and, therefore, our country.'

Anandi gazed at her father. She internalized the meaning of freedom—it was a responsibility. The seed of serving the nation was sown at that very moment.

Later on, this motto gave her a purpose in life. These were the tiny first steps towards her journey of becoming one of the most respected leaders in the history of Indian politics, and becoming the first woman chief minister of the state she was born in.

When her father went back to the fields, little Anandi sat in the kitchen with her sister Manguben in deep thought. She had learnt an important lesson that day. She had learnt about freedom and the value of serving the nation.

In early twentieth century, Jethabhai Patel wed Menaben, a local Gujarati girl, and taught her to read and write. When Anandiben was born in 1941, she joined her seven elder siblings: Saritaben, Keshubhai, Dev Chandbhai, Manguben, Chotu bhai, Chandubhai and Shantaben. Saritaben was the eldest and like a mother to Anandiben, considering the huge age gap. Later, Menaben gave birth to two more girls, Manguben and Lalita.

Anandiben recalls her mother as being an extremely loving person. She took good care of her family. She was a quiet woman, and she made sure every child knew household work, even things like how to make butter or pickle. She was very supportive and stood by her daughters-in-law in everything they did; there was a feeling of mutual respect.

Menaben was also an expert in making Ayurvedic *aushadhi*s (medicines) and took care of all animals. She actively encouraged Anandi and her siblings to study—having had an education, she understood its importance.

Anandiben clearly remembers how her parents never dissuaded her bhabhi's liking for tea. Making tea had been a new practice for her parents, but they accepted all rituals and customs that their daughters-in-law had brought along with them.

They were a big family of 12 members—the parents, brothers and sisters—in a three-room house made of brick and mud. She could never forget her single-storey house with lots of open space, wells, stables and pens. She describes that the house had a huge sitting room with an attached kitchen in the corner. There were two bedrooms. Her brothers mostly slept either in the open area outside the house or in the sitting room. The mud flooring was smooth and the windows were cut into the walls so that there was proper ventilation and the smoke from the cow-dung fire had the means to be let out.

Jethabhai was a man with a creative bent of mind and, over the years, he added new structures to the house. The family had a tradition of offering prayers before meals and the children would sing 'Mangal Mandir Kholo' with their father.

Agriculture was the primary occupation of the workforce in newly independent India. Villages tended to be self-sufficient as they grew their own vegetables and had a common well to collect water. Almost every household in the village had cows, hens and other domestic animals for fresh milk, eggs, etc. Their village had farmers, blacksmiths, carpenters and potters, among others. There was no electricity in most villages including Anandiben's and during the dry months, the women had to walk for miles to bring water.

Traditionally, the Indian villagers held a deep loyalty to their villages and so did Jethabhai. The Patel family had its roots deeply entrenched in the mystic charm and cultural diversities of village life. According to Anandiben, the Indian village life was a mixture of tranquillity, serenity, quietude and innocence. The numerous small and big fields, several rivers, the chirping of birds and greenery in abundance was delightful.

Since Independence, the agrarian society has also become the foundation upon which the economy of the nation has banked upon. A majority of the people living in India involved themselves in agriculture and associated industries and, thus, made the country one of the quickest-developing world economies. However, during British rule, India's villages and their economy encountered a crisis. The eighteenth-century industrial revolution also influenced the villages. The British East India Company had subdued local kingdoms and established its domination by the eighteenth century.

In the decades following the First War of Independence in 1857, civic society gradually emerged across India and witnessed the foundation of the Indian National Congress (INC) on 28 December 1885. The period after World War I witnessed the nationwide non-violent movements of non-cooperation and civil disobedience, led by Mohandas Karamchand Gandhi. At the local level, people like Jethabhai participated in the freedom struggle by spreading Gandhi's wisdom and values to others. He worked to educate the society and end caste-based discrimination.

Over the next decade, several incidents happened that created some political unrest in the country. Over 200,000 men from the British Indian army participated in World War II, the Congress gave its final push for non-cooperation and Muslim nationalism, led by the All-India Muslim League, reached its peak. When India got independence in 1947, the political tension that was already brewing in the background, escalated. The partition of the subcontinent into India and Pakistan did not help in any way. But people celebrated Independence in their own ways in their respective countries, as it was a hard-earned victory.

Celebrations in the Patel household began with a prayer at the dinner table. Jethabhai narrated the story of the Independence struggle to his children and wife, who were sitting in a circle. He told everyone about Nehru's speech, Gandhi's involvement and the path ahead that needed to be taken to build a new nation. The family was all ears, and Jethabhai's talk impacted them in various ways.

Jethabhai was very clear about educating all his daughters as he believed that an educated citizen would have the most effective impact on the nation's development. Anandiben was enrolled in a girls' school where she studied till Class III. A peculiar thing about this school was that all the girls dropped out after the fourth standard and focused on learning household chores or got married after a few years.

Jethabhai enrolled Anandi in the boys' school at Kharod village after meeting the headmaster and she studied here from Class IV to VII. Anandiben shares how she was the only girl when she joined and would sit separately in one corner. She would sometimes bunk classes to eat mangoes from the mangrove close to the school. She did her homework on the way back home; she would solve one problem, and then walk some way only to stop again and solve another problem.

One thing she specifically mentions is three to five boys would sit in another corner of the class and were not allowed to mingle with the rest of the students. She asked the schoolmaster about them, and were told that these boys was Dalits. This disturbed the young girl and she thought endlessly about what she could do to make everyone sit together without any division, be it girls or Dalits.

The term Dalit was in use as a translation for the British Raj census classification of 'depressed classes' prior to 1935. It was popularized by the economist and reformer Dr B.R. Ambedkar (1891–1956), who included all depressed classes, irrespective of their caste, under the definition of Dalit.

Ambedkar and Gandhi supported the Government of India Act, 1935, which introduced reservation for the depressed classes, now renamed Scheduled Castes (SC). Soon after 1947, India introduced a reservation system to enhance the ability of Dalits to have political representation, and to obtain government jobs and education. Anandiben learnt about these facts at a very young age and, later, strived to work towards the betterment of all the classes equally, unlike others, who used the issue to garner votes.

Meanwhile, Saritaben shifted to Visnagar with her husband and they became parents to two children. Marriages then were really simple and more of a family affair. In fact, Saritaben's marriage was another example of Jethabhai's forward and free thinking. She married a man of her choice at a time when marrying for love was not socially accepted, since it was expected that the children would marry whoever their parents chose. It began as a way of uniting and maintaining good relations between upper-caste families, and eventually, the system spread to the lower castes as well, with the same motive in mind.

Instead of following the futile rules of society, Jethabhai debated that if people could find a more educated and suitable man than the one her daughter had chosen, he would cancel the wedding. His confidence and logic made people realize that getting married for the satisfaction of society made no sense, especially since choosing a life partner is such an important decision. The *hast milap* ceremony of Saritaben was followed by garba or dandiya raas in the village. Anandiben was quite young when most of her elder siblings got married.

Anandiben's childhood was full of joyful memories along with awe-inspiring anecdotes that shaped her early years. However, on being asked to share an incident from her childhood, she narrates one that sends her into laughing fits. When she was six or seven years old, the siblings would play a game called *dhingla-dhingli lagna*, where they would divide themselves into two sides: the groom's and the bride's. The play included all the wedding arrangements and decorations in a small area of the farm by the bride's side while the groom's side came with the baraat.

Anindiben took pleasure in bridal adornment and would dress up her dolls as brides. Her brothers would make a temporary wedding venue with bamboo sticks and mud. On one such game day, Anandiben, Chandubhai and Lalitaben were on the bride's side and, as always, Anandiben got her doll ready for the ceremony.

'Something is missing,' Anandi said to Lalita, looking carefully at the bride.

'What? She has got lips, nose and eyes,' Chandubhai said as he adjusted the nose made with a bamboo sliver.

'But it is not perfect,' said a restless Anandi and took out a pair of scissors.

'What are you doing?' Before Lalitaben could complete her sentence, Anandi had snipped off her own eyebrows. The siblings were flabbergasted. They did not know how to react.

Anandiben calmly pasted the hair above her doll's eyes. 'Now it looks perfect,' she smiled and looked at her brother and sister, who were looking at her, mouths agape.

Her act was naïve but it also showed her determined side. She could have cut her hair but she went for her eyebrows, something that was actually missing on the doll. She was clear without an iota of doubt that what she was doing was right. She did not care about herself, only about completing the task to the best of her abilities.

Today, at 80, Anandiben laughs at this story from over half a century ago. She points at her missing eyebrows as her eyes twinkle, proudly carrying that memory from her childhood. It reflects the image of a charismatic leader, who is fearless and a perfectionist. The play-act ceremony took place as planned and Anandiben was scolded by her parents—she learnt that she needed to be careful while being fearless.

She goes on to remember how Jethabhai had unique ways of punishing the children. Sometimes when he would misjudge and scold them, he would immediately ask Baa to make halwa for everyone. He never hesitated in apologizing to the children. He believed in forgiving and seeking forgiveness.

If the siblings killed an animal or insect by mistake, Jethabhai asked them to fast for a day. Anandiben remembered fasting after she along with other villagers had defeated a wild fox who had been hurting people and destroying crops.

Another day of fasting etched in her memory was 30 January 1948, when Mahatma Gandhi was assassinated. Jethabhai asked the family to offer prayers and fast for a day. He also hosted a circle in the evening where he discussed Gandhi's life with the family.

Meanwhile, the members of the Rashtriya Swayamsevak Sangh (RSS) began to envisage the formation of a political party to take their ideology further. Shyama Prasad Mukherjee left the Hindu Mahasabha due to a conflict over permitting non-Hindu membership. The Bharatiya Jana Sangh (BJS) was consequently started by Mukherjee in collaboration with the RSS.

In 1952, India held its first general elections in which the BJS won three seats, with Mukherjee as one of the winning candidates.

After his death in 1953, RSS activists in the BJS edged out career politicians and made it a political arm of the RSS and an integral part of its family. In the second Indian general election of 1957, under the leadership of Jawaharlal Nehru, the Congress easily won a second term in power, taking 371 of the 494 seats while the BJS won only four seats.

∽

In 1956, Jethabhai sent Anandiben to Visnagar, where they joined the NM High School. She lived with Saritaben's family, who was working as a teacher, but everyone visited the village during weekends and celebrated festivals together.

Aninandiben built strong leadership qualities from her early years. She learnt what family meant and how it was to be together as one. She witnessed incredible teamwork—imagine all the siblings working together on farms, playing together, serving food to one another and taking care of each other, and the values this closeness instilled.

These years formed Anandiben's personality. She witnessed situations from scarcity to abundance. She knew how to react in moments of crisis. She knew how to be empathetic towards others. She saw a relational structure with stability. The values defined by her father made her stand strongly by her views despite other people's efforts to break through with opposing beliefs. It helped her make the right decisions, both personal and political.

She lived a life that was deeply rooted in values and traditions. She went through all the basic challenges a person goes through, and these myriad difficulties later enabled her to create schemes and processes for the people she governed. She had this wonderful knack for being able to connect with people from all social classes and considered everyone to be part of a bigger global family.

Her interactions with her father and elder siblings, and observing how they swore by values, such as acceptance, determination, kindness, patience and respect helped her evolve as a person and held her in good stead later on in life. She learnt how members of a community should value each person based on their individual contributions, character and abilities, as different as they may be. Stature, success and money didn't determine a person's self-worth or place in the community. It was an important lesson, one that could have been applied to her strong leadership.

How Education Shaped the Iron Lady

If we want to reach real peace in this world,
we should start educating children.

—Mahatma Gandhi

While in high school, Anandiben actively participated in sports. She fondly recollects the days when she was the only girl running on the ground since her school had only three girl students. She represented her school in various sports categories, won many competitions and also became a district-level champion. This is not to say that she was a bad student academically; in fact, she was exceptionally good—she was an all-rounder.

Anandiben had set a precedent for other girls in the area, and many families enrolled their girls in school after seeing her being able to balance academics and extracurricular activities so well. When more girls joined the school, they created a kabbadi team. They would practise with the boys and play against them. A few parents expressed their displeasure, but the school principal was adamant about the parents letting go of their orthodox mindset and allowing their children to choose their own path unhindered to make the country proud. Gradually, many girls began participating in sports events. Ishwar Patel, Anandiben's physical education teacher, was a stern and unerring man. He treated all students the same, irrespective of caste and gender. His goal was to enrol more and more students in sports.

Anandiben still remembers the day she was presented the Veer Bala award by the school trustees and government officials. For the first time, she was on stage amidst multiple rounds of applause and cheers. After that day, she was known across the school by all the students.

During this phase of her life, Anandiben lived with Saritaben and helped her with the household chores, and farming on the weekends and on vacations, apart from her studies and sports practice. The house in Visnagar was offered to them by Babubhai Shah, a close relative who also ran an ashram in the area. The house had two rooms with an attached kitchen and bathroom, and he had given the additional room on the terrace to Anandiben for studying. It was Visnagar where she watched her very first movie, *Kunwarbai Nu Mameru*, in a cinema hall. The memory still makes her smile.

Saritaben's husband died quite unexpectedly within a few years, leaving her with five children. She was 30 then, and her youngest child was only a year old. As soon as Jethabhai got the news, he hurriedly sent Keshubhai to Visnagar. There was a purpose behind sending him. Traditionally, widowed women, both young and old, were asked to denounce colourful saris, part with their jewellery and even shave their heads. Saritaben had long and beautiful hair, and Jethabhai wanted to make sure that she was not forced to do away with it.

Keshubhai managed to reach Visnagar before everyone else. Anandiben and Manguben were asked to be with the children. The villagers had completed the cremation preparations while her husband's family was urging Saritaben to undergo a series of rituals.

'We will not have Saritaben's head shaved,' Keshubhai announced. 'This is not right, and we do not support regressive rituals.' Everyone looked at him in amazement as Saritaben stood shivering beside her mother-in-law.

'But this is our culture. Sarita needs to shave her head,' someone from the crowd shouted.

'Okay. Take a strand of her hair, but she will not live like a deprived woman. She is educated and independent. This is what our father has taught us, and this is what he wants,' Keshubhai said.

Everyone agreed, albeit begrudgingly, and decided that the rituals would be conducted in a subtler way. Anandiben's stomach churned when she heard the single crisp snip of the blade, and watched a limp strand of hair fall from Saritaben's head. If she would have had to give up all her hair, it would have been a horrible sight to behold.

Anandiben proudly recollects how the ritual of shaving a widow's head lost popularity after that day, and eventually ended in their community. Anandiben's family had led by example.

There was also an incident where Jethabhai arranged a marriage between a widow, Gomtiben, and a widower, Vithalbhai, who lived near Saritaben's house in Visnagar. He planned the marriage against the wishes of the villagers since he knew that the young boy and girl had a long life ahead of them. He believed that no one has the right to decide what is right and wrong for us. He believed in the upliftment of society and this he did by imparting his knowledge and wisdom. This, in turn, helped eradicate many regressive societal traditions.

Another tradition followed in those days was getting married to distant relatives. In addition, there was the tradition of exchanging daughters between families. In Anandiben's family, too, this was followed when Dev Chandbhai's brother-in-law became Manguben's husband.

Jethabhai was known for his good deeds and high values. In 1958, someone from another village offered his widowed daughter's hand to Chota Lalbhai, the second youngest son of Jethabhai. The woman, Ichaben, had an elder sister and a younger brother, Mafat Lal. It was Mafat Lal who came to Jethabhai with a proposal to get Ichaben and Chota Lalbhai married. Mafat Lal was an educated young man pursuing a bachelor's degree in psychology. He went on to do a PhD in psychology later. He expressed how much he appreciated and respected Jethabhai's progressive thinking. He asked, 'Will you get your son married to my widowed sister?'

Widow remarriage was against societal norms, but Jethabhai accepted as he was impressed by Mafat Lal's words. But on the wedding day, Ichaben's father put forward a condition. He said, 'When we are giving our daughter, we need your daughter to get married to our son.'

This was meant for Anandiben. Saritaben and Jethabhai immediately refused since Anandiben was too young for marriage and was completing her education. They preferred to cancel Chota Lalbhai's wedding. Arguments ensued but, finally, Ichaben's father took back his words and Ichaben got married to Chota Lalbhai.

Anandiben completed her schooling with exceptional success. She was one of the brightest students in Gujarat, be it in academics or sports. She had an incessant aspiration to pursue higher studies, but did not have the courage to discuss it with her father as, until then, she had studied wherever her father had her enrolled in.

The day she graduated high school, she could not sleep. She tossed and turned in bed worrying about what life had in store for her. She wanted to pursue science. The next day, Saritaben informed Anandi that her parents were coming to Visnagar in a few days. She also told her that everyone had conveyed their congratulations and blessings for her high school results. Anandi kept her head down and focused on what her next steps should be. She was not one to lose herself in victories; she trained her sights on the next goal and how to move towards it. The next few days passed slowly in an anxious haze.

Jethabhai and Menaben were in Visnagar for another purpose. They, along with Saritaben, were scheduled to go on a train journey organized by the government. The trip was taking a few key farmers along on a month-long journey through different states of India. They left the next day, the topic of college having not been broached; Anandiben was quite upset.

The next day, her brother Dev Chandbhai came to Visnagar from Pilvai, a village in Vijapur Taluka under Mehsana district, where he had shifted with his family. He gave her a letter that Jethabhai had written to Dev Chandbhai a few days ago. The letter read:

Deva,

Tame kem chho (How are you)*? I hope you and your family are doing well. I am writing this letter to you regarding Anandi. She will be getting her high school results in a few days. As you have shifted to Pilvai, I want you to talk about her admission to MG Panchal College for Science, a new college in your district. I want Anandi to study science there and stay with you. We will also send Mangu with her. She can complete her schooling and then join Anandi in college. We are going on a month-long journey. I trust you will do what I have asked.*

Lots of love!

A teardrop rolled down Anandiben's cheek as she read the letter. She felt extremely blessed and grateful at that moment. Deep within her heart, she rebuked herself for worrying when Jethabhai was sure to have thought about her studies. Her heart was so full of joy that she ran to the kitchen and made some halwa and *thepla* for everyone in the house. She prayed to Goddess Ambaji and thanked her father.

Dev Chandbhai told her that she would be shifting with him to Pilvai within a few months. He worked as a gram sevak in Pilvai. MG Panchal College was established in 1960 by Uttar Purva Gujarat Uchch Kelavani Mandal, Pilvai, and was affiliated to Hemchandracharya North Gujarat University, Patan. It was the only tri-faculty college in the rural area of North Gujarat. The sisters moved to Dev Chandbhai's house, which was a two-room set with a small bathroom and kitchen in the corridor. Jethabhai had already visited Pilvai and enquired about the appropriate course. His determination to get a good education for his children was commendable. Though they never spoke to each other about this, it remains with her as one of the most sacred memories of her father.

Anandiben lived in Pilvai for the next three years and pursued her bachelor's degree in science. Just like in school, she was the only girl in her college too. Manguben got admission to high school and later joined Anandiben with a few more girls in the next batch. Anandiben's principal in college waived her fee as she was the only girl who had had the courage to join college. He offered her ₹125, which was the annual fee, as scholarship. It was another proud moment and Anandiben returned the money to her brother, who had paid it at the time of admission.

An interesting incident Anandiben narrates is that her father was approached by a few Congress leaders when she joined college. They tried to influence Jethabhai that Anandiben should join politics as she had a bright future. Jethabhai refused without giving it a second thought. He wanted her to focus on her studies, complete them and only then decide where she wanted to go in the future. She joined politics 25 years after this episode.

Being the only woman in college was not easy and Anandiben had to face her share of challenges. She mentions a few situations where she was teased by boys; some even behaved flirtatiously with her, shouting 'welcome' when she entered the classroom or scribbling 'how are you?' on her desk. She was uncomfortable in the beginning, but her goal was clear: to study and focus on her education. She reported the misdemeanours to the principal, who reprimanded the boys, explaining to them how teasing would only discourage girls from pursuing a college education.

Anandiben dealt with all the challenges and moved forward. She shares that she would sometimes push the troublemakers in the corridor out of frustration when they annoyed her, but that later they all became friends.

Anandiben represented her college in sports as well. She would go to Bharuch with all the boys to participate. She became a champion. It was a matter of immense pride. She would wake up at 4.00 a.m., complete the household chores, study and then practise her game. As other girls joined college, they started practising together to gauge each other's performance and level of preparation. Everyone would joust for the medals but, in the end, it was Anandiben who won most of them. It was as if a leader was being cultivated. Her achievements were bound to inspire more and more girls to stand up and participate, and they did.

Once, she had a conflict with a professor. He used to follow the girl students around and make them uncomfortable. He also used to harass girls when they travelled to other cities for competitions. When Anandiben did not pay attention to his actions, he tried to fail her in sports. He marked the wrong measurements in long jump and other track events. However, Anandiben always knew how to stand by what is right. She believed that if you have not done anything wrong, nothing or no one can put you down. She went straight to the office of the principal, M.S. Shah, and complained about the professor. The principal asked another professor to take her test in physical education and they found that the other professor had intentionally failed Anandiben. Observing this and his behaviour towards the other girls, the professor was promptly suspended.

In 1960, Bombay State was dissolved and split along linguistic lines, forming Maharashtra and Gujarat, after a series of violent protests. This was the post-Independence Nehruvian golden era. India's new youth culture had exploded and Indians had begun experimenting with informal western fashion. Secularism, socialistic economic practices based on State-driven industrialization, and a non-aligned and non-confrontational foreign policy became typical of the modern Congress party.

In 1961, the Indian Army marched into Goa and ejected the Portuguese. For the first time in 400 years, India was free from all foreign colonial domination. The country was pictured as an aeroplane poised for economic take-off. Following this, Jawaharlal Nehru won another landslide victory in the 1962 general election, his third and final election campaign. In these elections, the budding Jana Sangh won 14 seats.

As politics in India was witnessing changes, Anandiben's life, too, was about to take a turn. In 1962, the last year of her graduation, Mafat Lal was making great strides in impressing both Jethabhai and Dev Chandbhai in Pilvai. He talked much about education, among other things. Jethabhai had been noticing the young boy for the past four years and decided that he would get Anandiben married to him.

Anandiben came back from college one day to find her father, Keshubhai, Dev Chandbhai and Mafat Lal at home. She went to her room straight away and eavesdropped on their conversation. Some time later, Jethabhai called Anandiben downstairs and told her that they had fixed her marriage to Mafat Lal. He was, according to everyone, the most suitable boy for Anandiben. Little did they know how things would eventually turn out.

Setting the Stage

In doing something, do it with love or never do it at all.

—Mahatma Gandhi

In 1962, Anandiben married Mafat Lal. On the same day, at the same venue, Jethabhai got Shantaben, Manguben and Lalita married to their respective grooms. Anandiben was back at Pilvai the very next day. She also refused to take any dowry with her. She told everyone that her father had given her an education, which was her most prized possession and more valuable than any materialistic gift.

Jethabhai had spoken to Mafat Lal's family before the wedding that Anandiben would complete her education first and only then go to her in-laws' house. It was a bit difficult for the family to accept this but Anandiben was stubborn about completing her graduation.

She moved in with her husband to a separate house in Pilvai, where she continued to pursue her studies. Manguben, too, joined the same college. On the one hand, Anandiben was not very happy about getting married before she could complete her graduation. But on the other, she could not have refused her father's decision and knew that he must have given it much thought. Anandiben was 21 when she got married to Mafat Lal, who was at the time 25.

Mafat Lal was pursuing his bachelor's in arts then, a rarity in those days. This had impressed Jethabhai and he had not been able to say no to Mafat Lal's marriage offer. For Anandiben, however, it turned out to be a gut-wrenching decision. Mafat Lal and Anandiben did not share an affectionate bond. She began to wonder how she would maintain the relationship and keep her sanity at the same time. She struggled with thoughts of wanting to leave and prayed for the situation to get easier. There were times when Anandiben would seek love and care but all efforts to do so were thwarted. Mafat Lal's behaviour was not that of a responsible husband.

Anandiben's father sent the monthly ration from his farms and took care of other things. The days weighed heavy on her heart. She faced a couple of incidents where she felt humiliated. For a year, she tried to create an amicable relationship with her husband despite all the conflicts but nothing worked.

Anandiben could not study because she had to cook for Mafat's friends when they visited. Mafat Lal would not help her out with anything around the house. She had to do everything alone and realized that things were definitely not working out. She could not focus on her exams and decided to leave Pilvai.

One night, it was raining heavily as Anandiben sat by a small window in her house waiting for Mafat Lal. Finally, she wiped her tears and decided to leave for her father's house in Kharod. Before

Mafat Lal could reach home, Anandiben had left on a city bus.

Anandiben reached Kharod at midnight. Everyone was shocked to see her without Mafat Lal. Menaben came out running and asked her to get inside the house as it was raining heavily. Anandiben told everyone that she had come for a vacation. Jethabhai suspected that there was more to it than meets the eye, but he chose to keep that to himself.

Days passed and Anandiben didn't go back to Visnagar. She would sit alone for hours or work on the farms. Jethabhai was concerned as he could see that Anandiben was disturbed. He asked Menaben, but she was unaware of what was going on.

'*Mane vaat karva do* (Let me talk),' Jethabhai told Menaben and called for Anandiben. She tried to give excuses to avoid the conversation, but Jethabhai insisted and, after a point, she couldn't keep it from them anymore.

'*Su thayu* (What has happened)?' Jethabhai asked Anandi. They were both sitting on a cot near the animal pens.

'*Kam nahi* (Nothing),' Anandiben looked down and unfurled the threads in the cot.

'Chains do not hold a marriage together. It is threads, hundreds of tiny threads which sew people together through the years,' Jethabhai said as a lone tear rolled down Anandiben's cheek. 'I know your college has started, why are you not going back?' he spoke in his firm voice.

'I don't want to study,' Anandiben replied.

This response shook Jethabhai to the core. He knew this was the last thing Anandiben would say to him. 'Andi, tell me what happened?' Jethabhai kept his hand on hers and she burst into tears.

She told him about her marriage and the problems she had been facing over the past couple of months.

'*Tane su joichhe* (What do you want now), Andi?'

'I don't want to go back. I don't want to study,' she said, still looking down.

'*Tame chhodi mango chho* (You want to give up)? I thought education would change how you react to situations in life,' Jethabhai said.

Anandiben looked up and nodded in response.

Jethabhai took a heavy breath and said, 'OK, give up then! Did you give up when you were the only girl in your school? Did you give up when you were pulled down by people in college? Did you give up when you were asked to leave the sports ground? Give up all your dreams. Show all the women whom you have inspired until now that this is what happens to girls who get educated and empowered. After your separation, people will not send their daughters to school and college. They will think that if a girl gets an education, it becomes difficult for her to stay in a marriage,' he stood up. 'I will not force you to stay in a bad marriage, but I want you to try, like you have always done, Andi. Anandi never gives up, never loses faith, is always hopeful and endures through every circumstance. We have to become great forgivers to be great human beings. We have to deal with other people's imperfections. We cannot run away from our problems; we have to face them and move ahead in life. You need to fill in the gaps. Rest is your choice, Andi. This is your house, and you can stay here forever, but as a father, I want to see my daughter fight all odds and become an example to look up to. Stand against your partner if needed, we are all with you, but don't quit your education. What will you do in life?'

Jethabhai left without seeking any response. That night, Anandiben couldn't sleep.

The next day, she asked Chotu bhai to drop her back. She had decided that she would study and work. She decided to face all her problems and become an example for women who are tortured at home. She pledged to be an independent woman who stood for herself. Her father's firm words were the truth that finally allowed her to start loving herself. She shares this incident with a lump in her throat.

It was not a perfect start for Anandiben, but her father's words motivated her to get back on her feet. She still remembers each word very clearly. She went back and completed her bachelor's degree. In 1964, she graduated. At that time, the education sector in Gujarat was facing a huge crisis. There was no proper process to recruit teachers and professors. Another incident that she recalls is when, in 1962, she wanted to be a doctor, but could not pursue it due to her marriage and several other restrictions. Instead, she pursued a BSc.

Meanwhile, at the national level, Jawaharlal Nehru's death led to an internal crisis in the Congress. There were differences among the top brass of the Congress regarding the future of the party, which created a lot of issues within. K. Kamaraj as the 'kingmaker', and the defeat in the Indo-Chinese war of 1962 ensured the victory of Lal Bahadur Shastri over Morarji Desai as Nehru's successor. The Congress split into two parties: Indian National Congress (O) and Indian National Congress (R) as a left-wing/right-wing division.

On the other hand, the Jana Sangh also attracted many conservative Congressmen who were disenchanted with the policies and politics of Jawaharlal Nehru and the Congress socialists. The Jana Sangh's strongest constituencies were in Rajasthan, Gujarat, Maharashtra, Madhya Pradesh and Uttar Pradesh. The Jana Sangh leadership strongly supported a stringent policy against Pakistan and China, and were averse to the USSR and political communism in India.

At this time, far away from politics, Anandiben's life was going through constant ups and downs but, determined, she moved forward. Her relationship with Mafat Lal became stable as time passed. Anandiben looked for a job and found her first one with the Mahila Vikas Greh in Visnagar that involved working for the upliftment of women. There she taught vocational courses to more than 50 widows. She was soon appointed by the Vikas Greh Trust as a teacher, and was assigned the responsibility of teaching the women and taking care of the centre. Meanwhile, she decided to pursue an MSc (master of science) on the weekends. She shifted with her husband near Mahila Vikas Greh's office.

Anandiben shares a story about the issues the organization faced due to the non-release of government grants towards the Mahila Vikas Greh by the then Member of Legislative Assembly (MLA) Shantaben. Anandiben personally provided rations to the women from her salary and sometimes from her own kitchen. Anandiben met Shantaben to discuss the issues but to little avail. Totally helpless, Anandiben left the job. Mafat Lal was working at the NM High School then, and they had to return to her brother's place.

After a few days, the 50 widows from the centre came to her house and requested her to start teaching them again. 'Ben, you are our only hope. If we get a good education, we will be able to do something with our lives,' one of the women said, holding Anandiben's hand.

At that moment, her father's words echoed in her ears. He had told her that her education would be useful only if she shared it selflessly. Besides, it would give women of the society their deserved place.

In 1965, Anandiben agreed to rejoin the Mahila Vikas Greh. She taught women a course organized by the central government. It was during her stay at the Greh that she personally helped many girls and worked towards creating a better life for them.

Her duty hours were from 11.00 a.m. to 5.00 p.m. She contributed to the cause of women's education for the next one year. In 1965, her husband was called to Ahmedabad for a job, and without much ado, they packed their bags and moved again.She began looking for jobs.

One day she saw an advertisement in the newspaper about a position with the police department.The police uniform had always fascinated her, which is why she applied for the position. In fact, she even cleared the exam but faced resistance from her husband. That is when she decided to pursue her master's in science. After moving houses, they got to know that Mafat Lal's job was not permanent. Anandiben started taking tuitions in the nearby locality while continuing to pursue her MSc degree.

In 1965, when Anandiben was in her final year of her MSc, her son Shwetank was born. After a long time, there was cause for celebrations in the family. It became difficult for her to balance her post-graduation studies, take care of Shwetank and, after her sisters had convinced her to pursue a bachelor's in education (BEd). Around this time, a frightening incident happened. A day before her last MSc exam, her 11-month-old son, who was playing outside their home, mistakenly swallowed a pin. Anandiben ran to the hospital with Shwetank, whose mouth was covered in blood and he required stitches.

Anandiben couldn't clear her exams. As per the university laws, she had to pass all her exams in October. She was really upset about it, although glad that her son was out of danger. After a few days, Manguben also shifted to Ahmedabad with her family, and this was a huge support for Anandiben. Eventually, Mafat Lal's sister and Saritaben's daughter moved into their house. They then took care of Shwetank while Anandiben and Manguben together pursued their BEd degree.

The 1967 general election saw Indira Gandhi win, with Congress grabbing over 54 per cent of the seats. The Jana Sangh saw an upturn in its vote share and won 35 seats. The same year, Anandiben was in her second year of the BEd course. Her family's financial situation was not stable as Mafat Lal did not have a fixed income and, after having a child, their expenses had increased.

Anandiben began the search for a teaching job with renewed vigour. She found an advertisement in *Gujarat Samachar* about a requirement for a maths and science teacher in Mohinaba Kanya Vidyalaya at Ashram Road in Ahmedabad.

Anandiben was convinced that she might not be able to secure the job, but she went for the interview anyway. Up early and ready, she reached the school with her papers and saw that there was a long queue of male and female teachers who had come to interview.

Restless and anxious, she sat on a bench outside the reception area and waited her turn, checking her watch every two minutes.

'Anandiben Patel?' Someone screamed her name amidst the hopefuls crowding around the reception. Anandiben quickly stood up, adjusted her saree and went inside the principal's office. It was a big room full of books and trophies. A man in his 50s asked her to sit as he analysed her papers and adjusted his spectacles. 'Daulatbhai Desai, Principal', said the wooden nameplate on the desk.

'Anandiben, you have very good credentials in your school, a BSc degree, but you are yet to complete your BEd,' said Daulatabhai.

'Yes, sir, I am still studying, but I have sufficient experience for this position,' Anandiben uttered with confidence.

'Okay. Please take a mock lecture—teach one part of a chapter from both the math and science book. Which chapter would you like to teach in mathematics?'

'I will teach trigonometry.'

The principal was surprised as trigonometry was considered to be one of the toughest sections in mathematics.

'And I will teach chemistry in science.'

The principal took her to the class where she taught trigonometry with great clarity and focus. Daulatbhai was quite impressed to see Anandiben's confidence and passion.

After the lecture, Daulatbhai said, 'I have never seen a teacher pick trigonometry for a mock lecture. I must congratulate you!'

Anandiben smiled and asked, 'What about science?'

'I don't think we need to take that mock lecture. Please collect your appointment letter from my office.'

Daulatbhai walked towards his office, leaving behind a visibly relieved Anandiben. She wrote a letter to her father about the appointment and bought some sweets on the way back home. Jethabhai came to Ahmedabad with Menaben, where he was to attend a Bhagavad Katha event for a fortnight. He asked Anandiben if everything was fine in her married life and promised to share with her his learnings from the katha.

Anandiben joined Mohinaba Kanya Vidyalaya in 1967 as a mathematics and science teacher. Mohinaba was an all-girls private school in Ashram Road, Ahmedabad. Anandiben received a warm welcome from all her peers, educators and other staff members. Her life began to change for good thereafter. She soon became a mother for the second time. The family was blessed with an angelic daughter—Anar.

Anandiben became an experienced teacher and made some really good friends at school. Of all her colleagues, Charuben was the closest to Anandiben, almost like her younger sister. Daulatbhai Desai, along with the teachers, brought innovation to conventional teaching. This was the time when Anandiben began to get acquainted with the education techniques and processes that helped her later when she became the minister of education.

Today, she believes that after Jethabhai, it was Daulatbhai Desai who shaped her as a person. After learning values from her father, she learnt professional ethics from Daulatbhai. She also developed a deep understanding of the planning and execution of various methods involved in teaching students.

The students began their day with a prayer and a lesson from the history of the Indian freedom struggle. Six decades ago, Daulatbhai had worked with a vision similar to India's new National

Education Policy (NEP) introduced in 2020. The policy envisions an India-centric education system that seeks to transform our nation sustainably into an equitable and vibrant knowledge society. It raises the importance of mother tongue and regional languages. Daulatbhai always promoted the Gujarati language but never imposed anything. Priority was given to trips within and outside the state that encouraged exposure to activities that enabled all-round development. Activity-based learning was the focus of studies. The teachers gradually introduced subjects like speaking, reading, writing, physical education, languages, art, science and mathematics.

High-school education is intended to inculcate multidisciplinary study, coupled with depth and critical thinking. He aimed at making education more holistic. Students would visit NGOs and anganwadis to meet the beneficiaries and understand their problems at the grassroots.

Anandiben organized and attended all these tours. She visited Somnath, Rameshwar, Kutch and Jaipur. She particularly remembers a specific tour of Kashmir where she had to go for 15 days. Most of the female teachers had refused citing personal problems, but Anandiben, who was new and the mother of a two-year-old son, came forward. Daulatbhai gave Anandiben's example to all the teachers, and, finally, Meenakshiben Desai, the sports teacher, Chimanbhai and Charuben agreed to accompany her. They convinced more teachers to go on the trip and Daulatbhai, too, went with the students. She laughs now when she remembers that she had bought more than a hundred kilograms of dry fruits and gifts for the families of all students and distributed them in the train.

Anandiben shares her learning even today with the university vice chancellors of UP and Madhya Pradesh. Most of her teaching years passed in learning about the education system, travelling the country and taking care of her children. Her hard work was unmatched. She would work for more than 20 hours a day. She learnt discipline from Daulatbhai, who would reach the school premises before anyone else and leave only after all the staff members had left for the day. She closely observed and inherited his traits.

In 1974, tragedy struck Anandiben's life. Her father called everyone home and declared that he had decided to go for *santhara*, or *samadhi-marana*, a religious practice of voluntarily fasting unto death by gradually reducing the intake of food and liquids. In Jainism, this is a controversial religious practice in which a person stops partaking of food with the intention of preparing for death. Such persons withdraw all physical and mental activities right before going for santhara.

Everyone in the family was shocked and upset by this decision. Jethabhai asked everyone to continue doing whatever each of them was doing and leave him alone. He asked only Saritaben to stay with him until the end. He made a small hut for himself in the fields and started his practice. Anandiben visited home every two days during this time and sat with her mother for hours.

Saritaben did not leave Jethabhai alone even for a minute. She sat next to him, reading verses from the Ramayana. She lit a small lamp next to him in the evenings, when all the family members would come to see him. He was becoming weak with each passing day. One evening, Saritaben had to leave for Visnagar urgently. No one told Jethabhai that Saritaben had left Kharod for the night. That same night, Jethabhai renounced his body and became immortal through his values and actions. Anandiben shares that Saritaben always regretted going to Visnagar that night.

Jethabhai was a man who lived an inspiring life worth remembering. He was the man who nurtured one of India's greatest leaders—Anandiben.

In the world of politics, too, it was a tumultuous year: economic problems, corruption and the conviction of Indira Gandhi in electoral malpractice led to widespread protests against the Congress (R) government.

In 1975, Indira Gandhi declared a state of emergency and threw many major opposition politicians in jail including the leaders of the Jana Sangh. In 1977, the Emergency was withdrawn, and elections were held. The Jana Sangh joined forces with the Bharatiya Lok Dal, the Congress (O) and the Socialist Party to form the Janata Party (People's Party).

Indira and Sanjay Gandhi both lost their Lok Sabha seats. So did all the Congress candidates in the northern states such as Bihar and UP. The Congress was reduced to just 153 seats, of which 92 were from four of the southern states. The Janata Party's 298 seats and its allies' 47 seats (of a total of 542) gave it a massive majority and Morarji Desai became the first non-Congress prime minister of India. Former Jana Sangh leaders Atal Bihari Vajpayee and L.K. Advani became the external affairs and information and broadcasting ministers, respectively.

The new Janata-led government reversed many Emergency-era decrees and opened official investigations into Emergency-era abuses. The latter entailed detaining people without charge or notification to families; abusing them when they were in detention; and misusing public and private media institutions such as the national TV network Doordarshan for government propaganda. Although several major foreign policy and economic reforms were attempted, continuous in-fighting and ideological differences rendered the Janata government ineffective in addressing the problems of the nation.

By mid-1979, Prime Minister Morarji Desai was forced to resign and his successor Chaudhary Charan Singh failed to sustain a parliamentary majority. Indira Gandhi and her new Congress (I) party won the 1980 general election. The Janata Party dissolved in 1980 with the members of the erstwhile Jana Sangh reconvening to form the Bharatiya Janata Party or BJP—the party Anandiben would later become a key member of.

The Turning Point

The future depends on what you do today.

—Mahatma Gandhi

Public anger against the Congress and the Emergency enabled the Janata Party alliance to emerge victorious in the 6th Lok Sabha elections held in 1977. While the majority it bagged with the help of the coalition partners allowed a comfortable win, the equations within the coalition were getting increasingly unstable, which, coupled with other troubles, forced them to lose their grip on power.

A split in the alliance between the socialists and nationalists in 1979 led to members of the Bharatiya Lok Dal and the erstwhile Socialist Party withdrawing their support to the government. Prime Minister Morarji Desai resigned after losing a trust vote and Charan Singh was sworn in as the new prime minister in June that year. However, his position too could not be affirmed as the Congress backed out from its promise of support. As the government failed to prove its majority, Charan Singh resigned and the 7th Lok Sabha elections were announced for January 1980.

Indira Gandhi's leadership and the Congress faced formidable challenges from various regional and other prominent leaders of the Janata Party, such as Satyendra Narayan Sinha and Karpoori Thakur in Bihar, Ramakrishna Hegde in Karnataka, Sharad Pawar in Maharashtra, Devi Lal in Haryana and Biju Patnaik in Orissa. However, internal rifts between Janata Party leaders and the country's political instability tipped the scales in favour of Indira Gandhi's Congress (I).

Subsequently, the Congress swept 353 Lok Sabha seats while the Janata Party and the remaining alliance managed only 31. The alliance witnessed many more splits over the years but it had achieved one important landmark—that of being the first coalition party to govern India.

In Gujarat, too, the coalition worked. Babubhai Jashbhai Patel was the chief minister from June 1975 to March 1976 as the leader of the Janata Morcha, while his second stint from April 1977 to February 1980 was with the Janata Party.

The newly formed BJP with Vajpayee as its first president started to moderate the Hindu nationalist stance of its predecessor, the Jana Sangh, in order to gain wider appeal. It began emphasizing its links to the Janata Party and the socialist ideology.

While political history in India was clocking distinct changes, a huge change was taking place in Anandiben's life too. After her father's wilful passing away, her mother died due to cardiac arrest. Her motherhood was an example for many, especially Anandiben, who shares many stories about her mother pensively.

During that time, Gujarat society was divided in the wake of the KHAM (Kshatriya, Harijan, Adivasi and Muslim) revolution. In the Anand Lok Sabha constituency, caste-based politics had taken centre stage with both the major parties, the Congress and the BJP, setting their focus on the KHAM votes.

While not openly acknowledging the special attention they were paying to the KHAM group, the parties did recognize the electoral importance of this section. The concept of KHAM was evolved by Madhavsinh Solanki, congress leader and former Gujarat chief minister, in the 1980s to shift the power base from the upper caste, including the Patels and Brahmins, to minorities and other backward castes (OBCs).

Distinctions were being created between Hindu and Muslim areas. This was the decade where Anandiben's life took a huge turn. She had been teaching at Mohinaba Vidyalaya for a long time and around 1984, had become one of the senior-most teachers.

Meanwhile, Prime Minister Gandhi's younger son, Sanjay Gandhi, had died in an aeroplane crash in June 1980, which had led her to encourage her elder son, Rajiv, who was at the time working as a pilot, to enter politics. Gradually, Indira Gandhi's politics and outlook grew more authoritarian and autocratic, and she became the central figure within the Congress, with a focus on unprecedented centralization of power.

Indira Gandhi's assassination on 31 October 1984 by her bodyguards prompted the 1984 anti-Sikh riots, during which more than 3,000 people were killed. It also catapulted Rajiv Gandhi to the head of the Congress and eventually to the post of prime minister. The Congress won 414 Lok Sabha seats in a sympathy wave while the BJP, with just two seats, was still biding its time to attain a national presence. It was unable to perform in the Gujarat assembly elections too.

The following year, Anandiben's life, too, was poised for a sea change. Her school had organized an exposure visit for the students to Sardar Sarovar Dam, a concrete gravity dam built on the Narmada River in Kevadia near Navagam, Gujarat. Four Indian states—Gujarat, Madhya Pradesh, Maharashtra and Rajasthan—were slated to receive water and electricity supply from the dam. The construction work was still in progress. The teachers had taken more than 200 girls for the visit. When the bus reached the dam, the teachers instructed the students to stand in queue outside the bus.

Charuben Desai divided the girls into groups of 25 and assigned one teacher to each group. The groups moved to the different parts of the dam site. The view was beautiful, with mountains all around and gushing water. The river flow had been diverted as construction work was about to begin. Students were excited to see the workers digging through the mountains. A few girls went to sit on the edge of an uneven wooden plank, facing the river.

The PT teacher saw this and blew his whistle to alert the girls; instead, they jumped and ran after each other. Before the PT teacher could reach the girls, one of them slipped into the water. The other girls began to scream in fear and it was their screams that caught everyone's attention. In the ensuing chaos, before anyone could help, another girl slipped away into the water.

Without delay, Anandiben ran towards the accident site. She saw both the girls struggling in the water. She looked around for a second, tied the pallu of her saree around her waist and stepped down, towards the river.

'Calm down and try to swim towards me,' Anandiben coaxed the girls as she extended one hand and held onto the rocky, slanting bank with another. Fortunately, the water had a slow current and the girls could swim towards Anandiben.

'Hold my hand,' she directed Niranjanbhai as the other teachers joined in. He held Anandiben's hand while she stood firm in the water with one hand extended towards the girls. She rose like a bridge to pull the girls to safety.

One of the two girls managed to hold Anandiben's hand. Now, the challenge was to grab the second girl's hand. Anandiben did not break the chain and asked the first girl to hold the other girl's hand so both could be pulled in together.

'When she comes upwards, grab her hand,' Anandiben hollered.

The other girl slowly came near the corner and both of them held each other's hands tightly. Everyone sighed in relief and pulled Anandiben. After relentless efforts from Anandiben and the supporting team, the girls were successfully pulled out. Anandiben could've slipped in the water, too, but she displayed immense courage and risked her own life to protect the girls. The gathering had witnessed an act of bravery and selflessness. Anandiben and the girls were covered in bruises, and staff immediately attended to the victims and gave first aid to Anandiben. She had blood on her knees and elbows.

'I am fine, please, look after the girls,' she said and heaved a sigh of relief.

A local doctor was called in to make sure the girls were fine, which they were. The trip was abandoned and all the girls were asked to get back on the bus. Anandiben met both the girls and asked if they were alright.

'Thank you, madam, for saving our lives,' one of the girls said.

'God saved us,' Anandiben replied. 'You should have been mindful of what you were doing and of each other. This is what happens when we do not obey elders and do not take responsibility. Make sure something like this never happens again, and don't share this with anyone.'

Anandiben knew that if the news broke, there would be trouble for the school authorities and the staff members. She wanted to inform the principal personally. The students were asked not to create any confusion or panic and refrain from saying anything to their parents back home.

People who knew about this incident praised Anandiben, although she did not inform her own family about it. The trip organizer told Anandiben that a few days back, two boys had drowned in the river in a similar accident. No one had tried to save them. She had been courageous enough to risk her own life and save the students.

Finally, things settled down and the incident was not discussed any further. Principal Daulatbhai praised Anandiben for her actions but asked her to be more careful in future. He asked her for an event report nonetheless.

Back home, Mafatbhai had joined the BJP by this time. He was regularly attending *prachar* (promotions) with other party workers at different places in Ahmedabad. He was also present at lectures and rallies attended by senior BJP leaders.

The year 1985 was also significant for another event among the BJP ranks. Since the 'emergency' period, which had started in 1975, Narendra Damodardas Modi had been working in various capacities for the RSS division in Gujarat and later in Delhi. From coordinating opposition and organizing demonstrations to going underground and travelling in disguise, safeguarding political refugees and, finally, researching and writing the RSS's version of Emergency history in Delhi, Modi had made leaps within the RSS cadre. Then in 1985, the current prime minister of India was assigned by the RSS to BJP Gujarat.

Gujarat was plagued by riots over reservations. The law-and-order situation was slowly breaking down in the state and businesses were shutting down due to unending violence. Soon, the army was seen patrolling the streets of Ahmedabad. During this time, the BJP began emerging at the state level. It had won control of Rajkot and Junagadh in the municipal elections.

Within a short span of time, the party witnessed Modi's potential. He started with the Nyay Yatra (journey for justice). Mafatbhai was one of the promoters of the rally in Ahmedabad. Modi was actively looking for courageous, dedicated and educated team members to join the party. At this opportune time, the news of Anandiben's act of bravery broke out.

Gujarat Samachar published an article about the incident, and Anandiben's bravery became the talk of the town, and it reached Modi's ears. Anandiben was surprised to see the article. She had not wanted the news to break out. During BJP promotions, Mafatbhai would take Anandiben along, and she would motivate the women and promote education for girls. She delivered lectures and also taught children for free. Mafatbhai took Anandiben along for the Nyay Yatra as well, where party workers were to visit the villages across the state. The mission was to make the Gujarat government aware of the issues in the villages, such as drought conditions, etc.

The yatra was a huge success for Modi and planted the seed for BJPs growth in the state. That was the first time Anandiben saw Modi giving powerful speeches to the villagers. She also did research work with other party workers in the district regarding the drought issues as assigned by Modi.

After *Gujarat Samachar*'s article, Anandiben received several awards. She was felicitated with the Gujarat government's bravery award and the Charumati Yoddha Award. She came to be recognized across the state for her bravery and received many accolades in her school.

One evening, Anandiben was at home and her children, Shwetank and Anar, were studying in the verandah when Modi arrived. She was taken aback by his surprise visit. She came out and greeted him with folded hands.

'Namaste,' Modi responded.

Anandiben invited him inside the house. 'Shwetank, Anar, come inside,' the kids came inside and greeted the guest.

'*Tamne ahi ava maate sum banave chhe* (How come you are here)?' asked Anandiben and offered a glass of water from her open kitchen. 'Have you come here to meet Mafatbhai?'

'I have come to meet you, ben,' Modi smiled and continued, 'I saw you at the Nyay Yatra. I heard you talking to the women. It was so inspiring. You motivated so many girls by speaking about them getting an education.'

Anandiben nodded, still puzzled at Modi's presence in her home.

'What do you do otherwise?' he asked.

'I teach maths and science at a school. I tutor privately too.'

'Who takes care of the children then?'

'I have my sister-in-law and my elder sister's daughter who live here with us,' she replied, completely confused with the questions that were being asked. 'I will make you some tea,' Anandiben added quickly and went to the kitchen. She had some time to think while she prepared the tea and thepla. They had a wholesome conversation about the party, and its vision and upcoming plans. All the while, Modi did not share any particular agenda for his visit.

'May I take your leave now?' he said finally, and caressed Anar's head.

'Okay. Namaste,' Anandiben said and folded her hands.

Later in the evening, Anandiben asked Mafatbhai if he knew something about the visit but he told her that he had no idea.

At Mohinaba Kanya Vidyalaya, Daulatbhai Desai was retiring from his position. Anandiben found it hard to bid adieu to Daulatbhai, as she had been impacted the most by his persona, his style of working and his view on holistic education. The trustees had a meeting to recruit a new principal, and Sonal Desai's name was suggested by Mayaben, who was one of the trustees of the school.

The teachers had a meeting and discussed that someone from the school should become the principal instead. Besides, they were also wary of Sonal Desai's authoritarian behaviour. The teachers decided that Sudhaben should apply for the position as she was one of the senior-most teachers, and had good merit and credentials. In comparison with Sonal Desai, however, everyone realized that Sudhaben's credentials were lacking, and hence, there were chances that the committee would select Sonal Desai.

A senior clerk, Nattubhai, suggested Anandiben's name as she had better credentials and merit performance than Sonal Desai.

She resisted initially, but, persuaded by her colleagues, applied for the position.

'I am applying because you all are asking me to do it. But let me tell you, if I become the principal, everyone will have to work harder,' Anandiben declared as everyone laughed. The entire staff was in support of her leading the school.

The government selection committee came from Baroda. Senior educationist Leelaben, DO Rathore and Officer Brahambatt joined Mayaben for the interview. They were well aware of Anandiben's educational background and social work experience.

Mayaben was not in favour of recruiting Anandiben. When the committee asked Mayaben the reason for her statement, she responded, 'Anandiben will not listen to us and she will work in her own way.'

'But she has very good skills, she has credentials, we should consider her,' the committee members responded and scheduled Anandiben's interview. As Anandiben entered the room, the committee greeted her. The interview began and they had a long conversation about Anandiben's vision and plan of action.

'Also, we have feedback about you that you do not listen to others.'

'I don't mind listening. But I will not do anything wrong if anyone asks me to. I will do what is right and work in favour of the students and teachers,' Anandiben replied with confidence and looked at Mayaben from the corner of her eye.

'Will someone ask her to do anything wrong?' the committee asked Mayaben.

'No, no!' Mayaben was baffled.

'There's no other candidate who has a better plan and vision or experience than you,' Leelaben told Anandiben. 'Please, accept your appointment letter. All the best!'

Anandiben Patel became the new principal of Mohinaba Kanya Vidyalaya. Everyone in the school was ecstatic, be it the students or her fellow teachers. All the people admired her as they had seen her work in the past two decades. Meanwhile, Anandiben's son Shwetank was in Bangalore (now Bengaluru) for his graduation, while Anar was completing her schooling in Ahmedabad. At the time, Anandiben stopped tutoring privately because she had made sufficient arrangements for Shwetank's college fees. She was looking forward to her new role as the school principal.

Meanwhile, Modi counselled Mafatbhai, who was then a party worker, that Anandiben should join the BJP. He said that educated and empowered women such as Anandiben would motivate more women to join the BJP. Modi's vision was to expand the roots of the party and take it to all the villages and cities of Gujarat. He was full of ideas and techniques. He knew that Anandiben was a Patidar from North Gujarat and educated enough to push women to achieve bigger things.

He asked Mafatbhai to schedule a meeting with Anandiben where Modi and Shankersinh Vaghela, who was then general secretary and president of the BJP in Gujarat, would be present. Modi informed Vaghela about the meeting with Anandiben.

Mafatbhai took Anandiben to the meeting without sharing the agenda with her. He thought that if Anandiben joined politics, he would also get a chance to meet people at the national level.

Modi and Vaghela met Anandiben at the Income Tax Circle

in Ahmedabad. Anandiben was surprised to see Vaghela, the party president.

'Namaste,' Modi greeted Anandiben and introduced her to Vaghela.

Vaghela praised her for her bravery in the Sardar Sarovar incident and her contributions towards the promotion of women's education in the BJP.

'Anandiben, we think you should join the party. Right now, we are emerging as a unit and we need people like you. You have all the potential to become a great leader and take the party forward,' Modi said.

'Yes, she will join,' Mafatbhai said as Anandiben looked at him.

'I have an eight-hour job. I have children and I have household work. I don't think I will have time for party work,' Anandiben replied.

'We don't need your time. We just need your name,' Modi said.

'But I can't join politics,' she replied and elbowed Mafatbhai, who was about to interrupt.

'Anandiben, you are an educated woman. If women like you do not stand up for other women, if women like you do not promote girl education, if women like you do not encourage women to stand up for their rights, then what's the point of your education?' Modi said. He was firm in his resolve; the man who is known as one of the most influential and convincing leaders of the world had, and continues to have, the power to drive any individual from 'no' to a 'yes'.

His words were so precise and all-pervasive that the command in his voice struck a chord with Anandiben. What she could remember of that moment were the words from her father, who always told her to learn and share knowledge. He always wanted his daughter to become an example for the world.

Without thinking for another second, Anandiben said, 'Yes, I will.'

Amidst uncertainties and qualms about the system of political parties, one of the most dignified and compassionate leaders was born. When Anandiben started leading a public life, she put in a lot of hard work with sincerity and dedication, and began to emerge as a strong leader in BJP circles. For this reason, Modi appointed Anandiben as the president of the Gujarat Pradesh Mahila Morcha in 1987.

At the time, Modi was the maha mantri of the BJP in Gujarat. He suggested Anandiben organize a protest rally against the increasing inflation rate in India because it majorly impacted women. Anandiben planned to start the rally from the BJP office and walk to the Khadi Gramodyog office with a group of women raising slogans.

Anandiben mobilized over 700 women who marched in protest with flags and posters in hand. Under the leadership of Anandiben, the women walked with such enthusiasm that they managed to scare the local police. In no time, the police interrupted the peaceful protest and started lathi charging the women. While protecting the women from being hit, Anandiben got badly hurt. She was hit on the hand. The women and Anandiben were taken to a nearby hospital, where first aid was administered. Anandiben's hand was bleeding profusely, and she couldn't move it, yet she remained concerned about what had happened to the other women. It turned out that Anandiben's hand was fractured and the doctor advised rest.

'For how long will I not be able to move my hand?' she asked, wiping the sweat on her forehead with her working hand. Nobody in the family knew that this had happened to her.

'A minimum of three months; the hand will have to remain in a plaster cast.'

Anandiben was shocked. She could not afford to restrict the movement of her hand. Be it teaching, working or cooking, she needed her mobility back. She went home with the plaster and the children were really concerned. Her husband did not pay much attention when he got to know how it had all happened.

On the one hand, people were praising her bravery and courage and, on the other, her personal life was going through turmoil. In her Ahmedabad house, she slept on the ground floor while her son and daughter-in-law slept on the first floor.

One night, Anandiben was sleeping when her husband asked her to go and sleep on the first floor. She could not understand why he had asked her to shift, knowing very well that she would not be able to move because of her fractured hand. He forced her to go upstairs. Anandiben couldn't do or say anything and went upstairs to sleep.

The next morning she got a call from her daughter. 'Mummy, have you read today's newspaper?'

'No, I have not.'

'Please go and read it now,' Anar said and disconnected the call.

Anandiben ran downstairs and realized that Mafatbhai was not at home. She could not find the newspaper anywhere. She asked her neighbour for their copy. She could not believe her eyes. Mafatbhai had given an interview in which he had said how the BJP had given special importance to Anandiben and neglected him. He had also demeaned the protest organized by Anandiben. With this article, Mafatbhai had made evident the kind of pushback women face from their partners when they step out of domestic life.

Mafatbhai had said many negative things about Anandiben in that interview. His article was well-timed because there was a Mahila Morcha meeting scheduled for the same day.

Anandiben made an appointment and rushed to the office of the editor. She went inside the cabin and kept the newspaper on his table.

'What happened, madam?' he asked.

'Do you verify what you publish in your esteemed newspaper? Don't you think it's your responsibility also to ask the perspective of the person against whom you are publishing an article?' Her voice was firm.

'I am sorry, madam. I understand your point. We request you to give your statement so that we can publish it,' the editor stood up with folded hands.

'I will not give any justification to false allegations. Do you write and publish whatever you feel is right?'

Around the same time, Mafatbhai was encouraging all relatives and friends to read this article. But people could see how different the personalities of Mafatbhai and Anandiben were and why Anandiben was being given importance over her husband by the party's senior leaders. When Anandiben reached home, she saw her father and children sitting in the room. Anandiben was angry but she did not say anything.

'We all know Papa troubles Mummy, but this time he has crossed all limits,' said Anar.

'I have decided that I will not keep any relationship with him. I will never speak to him. We will stay in the same house, but there will be no communication.' She looked at her children. Mafatbhai did not say anything and left the room.

After this incident, household expenses were divided and the household ran according to the needs of the individuals. This was the most critical stage in Anandiben's personal life. Decades have passed but Anandiben has not spoken to her husband since that day, and has lived separately under the same roof.

Mafatbhai continued to be associated with the party. He filled out the application form as a gram panchayat member and fought the election. Anandiben would go on field visits to different villages and urge people to vote for him. This was the first time Anandiben asked people for votes that too for someone else.

Around this time, an incident took place that reiterates how decisive and strong Anandiben is as an individual. Mafatbhai's brother Dashrath was unable to get married as he was suffering from a mental health problem. Everyone knew about it. Mafat wanted to get him married off and believed he would become alright after marriage. But he couldn't have been more wrong!

There was an ashram, Mahipat Ashram, where Anandiben's sister and brother-in-law were teachers. Mafat Lal would go there to give weekend classes. There was a girl called Smita in the ashram who was known to all of them and Mafat wanted her to marry Dashrath. Anandiben was strictly against it. She told him that the marriage would ruin Smita's life, but they were adamant that the marriage should take place. He got a fake health certificate made for Dashrath and got both of them married. They shifted to Kalol, and Dashrath started working. When Anandiben and her sister went to Kalol to check if everything was fine, even before they could actually plan a visit to Dashrath's house, they got a call from the ashram that Smita had returned. Somehow, Anandiben had known this would happen.

The caretaker of the ashram, Sarojben, called Anandiben's sister Mangu. Mafatbhai asked Anandiben to go to the ashram. There they heard that Dashrath had physically abused Smita. Anandiben took Smita to her house. She convinced Smita to get a divorce and remarry. In time, Smita got married to someone who took her to the United States of America. Anandiben was glad that she had stood by Smita during troubled times and helped her secure her future.

In the Thick of It All

Be the change you wish to see in the world.

—Mahatma Gandhi

Modi was assigned the responsibility of organizing the BJP's campaign in the Ahmedabad municipal elections of 1987. He created a team to propagate the BJP's message and having a courageous woman leading the Gujarat Mahila Morcha was an added advantage.

He introduced Anandiben to all the women members of the party and felicitated her at the party office in Ahmedabad. He told everyone about Anandiben's knowledge and experience. He also declared that she would be leading as the president of the Mahila Morcha.

Among other reasons, Anandiben joined the BJP due to the party's dedicated efforts and groundwork for the rights of the community. The party has believed in noble work for society since its inception. As Anandiben was already involved with social work, she could see herself working with the people under the aegis of the BJP.

In keeping with her characteristic trait of taking initiative in every field she worked in, Anandiben asked Modi for the responsibility of mobilizing women from Ahmedabad. Instead, Modi trusted her with the responsibility of doing so for the entire state.

Until 1987, the Gujarat Mahila Morcha had just been a group registered on paper without any activity or agenda. Anandiben had to start from scratch. She began designing a strategy with Modi. From the very first day, he guided her in all areas of work. He asked her to create a list of districts and a comprehensive survey form. Anandiben did the BJP Gujarat Mahila Morcha work over the weekends. On weekdays, she would strategize innovative plans for education, and on weekends she started visiting districts near Ahmedabad.

She would go to a village, talk to the women about the issues they face, and then make a list of those who were interested in coming forward to do something constructive for society. Anandiben visited anganwadis and talked to the teachers and other staff as well. She also spoke to the male members of the villages to garner their support for the promotion of education for the girl child. Simultaneously, she was also given another task—to register more women members and to expand her team, and she did it dedicatedly.

At their meetings, Modi would share his learnings and research with Anandiben. He would ask a lot of questions and guide her with correct solutions. That was the time when the BJP was establishing its hold in Gujarat. The people there had not seen any development in the several years of INC rule. To the BJP's credit, they worked with people at the grassroots. So, rather than just promising solutions, they executed plans and presented the solutions. This approach really worked for the party, and it slowly became a huge support for the people.

After Jethabhai and Daulatbhai, it was Modi who influenced Anandiben's character and created a positive impact on her personality. He made her a compassionate leader who listened to everyone and worked with honesty. He taught her the importance of integrity at work and the true value of selfless service. Anandiben saw Jethabhai's reflection in Modi as it was all about the values of Gandhi and working for the welfare of the people. That was the dharma he infused in all the party workers.

At times, Anandiben's visits to different villages would not fructify; sometimes the women did not entertain her and at times the message did not get across. She would get upset with these responses, but Modi impressed upon her that nothing in life worked out without consistent efforts. He told her that she should continue her work with sincerity even if she was all alone.

Modi often sent her his research papers. Anandiben would attentively listen to his briefs about the sangathan. As Modi had instructed her to go on even if no one came—she had to do her work and get as many people as she could into the fold—she visited all the districts of Gujarat. Anandiben set an example with her perseverance, by registering 14 lakh members with a detailed survey. That was her first milestone that was recognized by the national leaders of the BJP.

She was called to present the survey report at an all-India BJP meet. Modi, in particular, was really proud at that moment. Anandiben went on stage and was awestruck looking at the thousands of people who had gathered for the event. Senior BJP leaders like Vajpayee, Advani and Murli Manohar Joshi were part of that meeting.

'Namaste, brothers and sisters. I am Anandiben Patel, president of the Gujarat Pradesh Mahila Morcha. I feel extremely proud to inform you that we have established a network of more than 14 lakh women with their detailed need analysis. We compiled a survey about their health, education, rights, finances, family planning and occupation.'

She confidently carried on and explained her methodology. She also acknowledged the support Modi had given to the project and her. The leaders and party members were amazed to see this confident woman on stage, delivering each word with so much conviction. That was another milestone for Anandiben, who was working day and night to balance her personal life, school and party work.

Her daughter Anar recalls that their father, Mafatbhai, always felt that Anandiben should manage the household and earn for the family, more so when she began to gain name and fame in the party and also became the Mahila Morcha president. Thankfully, the party did not support Mafatbhai because he was not a promising candidate.

After the event was over, Vajpayee personally praised Anandiben. She fondly remembers how he patted her back and motivated her to continue her dedicated work. That gave her the strength to serve more. Vajpayee was among the founding members of the Jana Sangh and had been a minister of external affairs (1977–79). When the BJP was formed in 1980, he was its first president and was elected to the Rajya Sabha in 1986.

The sustained efforts of Modi and leaders like Anandiben brought victory to the BJP in the municipal elections. Once Advani became president of the BJP, the RSS decided to place its members in important positions within the BJP. Given Modi's exemplary work during the Ahmedabad elections, he was elected organizing secretary of the BJP's Gujarat unit in 1987.

Anandiben, while handling her school duties, started actively working for the Mahila Morcha. She started travelling across the state, and soon, people got to know her and began to recognize her. She would go to places like Mehsana, Sabarkantha, Patan, Anand and Kheda and host sharing circles with the women there. She would also travel to faraway places like Kutch and Junagadh on the weekends. Modi would inform the local party workers about her visits and make all the arrangements. Sometimes, in some distant places like Bhuj, she would only reach by midnight and had to arrange everything by herself. It showed her sheer commitment towards her work. Her life was all about work, and sometimes her personal life was impacted, but she always made sure her kids were well taken care of. Surprisingly, Shwetank and Anar took good care of their mother and would often make halwa and chai for her when she returned home after a hard day's work. Anandiben inherited several of these family values from Jethabhai and Menaben, and she was more than happy to pass them on to her children.

One incident that reinforces Anandiben's decisive character, and also indicates her strong inclination towards her father's values and principles is when she stood against her own brother. He was getting his minor son married. But Anandiben intervened and stopped the marriage from taking place. She even threatened to call the police.

Anandiben said, 'I will call the police if you go ahead with this marriage. This is what our father has taught us and I will stand by his teachings.'

'What you are doing is not right, Andi,' her brother said.

Thankfully, the bride's family understood where Anandiben was coming from and called off the wedding for a year, until the groom was of marriageable age. A child marriage was averted because of Anandiben's efforts. This incident spoiled her relationship with her brother for a while, but she stood by her ideals, which she had inherited from Jethabhai.

Anandiben smiles when she thinks back to Modi's cheerful nature and remembers how he would crack jokes. One moment he would be asking intense questions about education, and the very next moment, he would make you laugh. He never made work feel like a burden. He always said that it is our prime duty to serve India and only then think about ourselves. He prepared everyone for both success and failure. He often told a frustrated Anandiben to be confident and start with 10 women, assuring her that it would soon be 10,000.

When Anandiben returned from her village tours, Modi asked for detailed survey reports. He would personally check the report of each district and ask detailed questions. For instance, he even asked how many of the women had black hair and how many had white! He wanted more and more young women to join the revolution of change he had envisioned for Gujarat.

Many of Anandiben's ex-students living in different districts across the state recognized her and joined the movement. Many girls who had been taught by Anandiben became mayors and councillors. They then supported Anandiben's initiatives in their districts. From fighting against child marriage to dowry, Anandiben always stood for the rights of women.

Among the many anecdotes from these times, she shares a disturbing incident from a time when Viramgram district was hit by the bird flu. Anandiben, along with other party members, was visiting the local hospital where they saw many stones kept in a huge ground. On further investigation, it came to be known that below the stones were the bodies of children who were affected by the flu. The hospital did not have enough facilities to treat the patients and simultaneously handle the epidemic in the district. The incident shook everyone. Anandiben helped the local citizens by appealing to government officials to take strong action but there was no response. She later escalated the issue in the press and filed a case. The INC government eventually had to send doctors and improve the medical facilities. The villagers thanked Anandiben for saving their children's lives.

For the next few years, Anandiben's efforts and work as the president of Gujarat Mahila Morcha were praised by party members, senior leaders and the people alike. People started to recognize her while her husband continued as a district head. She also started working at Dharti Vikas Mandal, a non-governmental organization (NGO), where she worked for many years on the ground and solved the issues of the people of several districts.

In 1990, the Ram Rath Yatra, a political and religious rally, was organized by the BJP and the Vishva Hindu Parishad (VHP). It was led by the then BJP president, L.K. Advani, to re-establish the Ram Temple at the Babri Masjid site. The rally started from Somnath in Gujarat. Anandiben had shown great expertise in mobilizing women, and hence was given the responsibility by Modi to get more women to join the rally from Somnath and other areas of Gujarat. Thousands of women under the leadership of Anandiben joined the Rath Yatra.

The Advani-led procession involved thousands of kar sevaks and volunteers from the Sangh. The journey started from Somnath on 25 September 1990, and passed through hundreds of villages and cities where organizers like Anandiben managed the crowds. The yatra covered a distance of 300 kilometres each day. Both Modi and Advani addressed public rallies that led to an outpouring of sentiment among Indians, and it became one of India's biggest mass movements.

As the yatra passed through Bihar, the state government arrested Advani. In Uttar Pradesh too, 150,000 yatra supporters were arrested by the government but still, tens of thousands of activists reached Ayodhya. Anandiben was appreciated for her efforts during the yatra for organizing and managing women from Somnath to Udaipur. That very year, the BJP withdrew its support to the government and led to an early call for parliamentary elections. The following elections saw significant gains for the BJP, both at the national and state level. Another prominent memory of the time spent working as the Mahila Morcha president was the Ekta Yatra in 1992. That decade was a new beginning of Anandiben's political journey. She had been working for the party for five years. The leaders had seen her commendable work and commitment.

The early '90s started with a very tough period in the political history of independent India. India faced many conflicts across its states from east to west, north to south, yet the power at the Centre sat as a mute spectator to this disintegration. Gujarat, in those days, was often under 'curfew'. It became a common word and occurrence in the state. Divisive politics was ruling the nation, and this vote-bank politics pitted family against family, and communities against communities.

Still, there was one man who lived up to the vision of Sardar Patel for a united and strong nation, committed to the values of Gandhi, and that man was Narendra Modi. The dark political scenario sparked Modi's patriotism and he gave his best. He worked very hard with leaders like Advani, Murli Manohar Joshi, Amit Shah, Rajnath Singh, Anandiben, and others. By then, Anandiben had established herself not only as a dedicated worker but also an efficient organizer. She rose to the occasion with Modi, challenging the unhealthy political status.

The last decade had turned Jammu and Kashmir (J&K) into a full-fledged battlefield. The opportunistic politics of the Congress party during the 1987 state elections had made J&K a hotbed of anti-India activities. The Valley that had once been called 'paradise on earth' was slowly becoming a warzone as blood spilt on the streets almost every day. The conflict reached such a stage that even the hoisting of the Tricolour had become taboo in Kashmir. Ironically, rather than taking strict resolving actions, all that the Congress did was watch helplessly.

This situation of systematic denigration of India's supremacy was unacceptable to the BJP. It was this same Kashmir that had called

Shyama Prasad Mukherjee to action and now it was time for the BJP to pick up the cudgels in favour of national unity. The Ekta Yatra was the response launched by the then party president, Murli Manohar Joshi. The yatra started from Kanyakumari, the place where Swami Vivekananda had found the purpose of life and was to end with the hoisting of the Tricolour at Lal Chowk in Srinagar.

The responsibility of organizing the yatra had been assigned to Modi, keeping in mind his well-established organizational skills. He made elaborate arrangements, along with active members like Anandiben, in a very short span of time, braving the huge risks that came with it. Anandiben worked without any fear, she visited every place that the yatra would cover, encouraging women across the nation to join the movement.

Under the guidance of Modi, she galvanized into action and inspired her fellow party workers, creating a patriotic fervour and awareness among them, thus laying the foundation for the yatra's success. In this process, she had not only shown that she had leadership instincts, but she had also exhibited the ability to deliver in any circumstance at a remarkable pace—a rare virtue in public life today. Modi now saw Anandiben as the quick decision-maker who performed well even in adverse conditions, which gave him the confidence to rely on Anandiben in the future.

The Ekta Yatra commenced on 11 December 1991, coinciding with the birth anniversary of Subramania Bharati and the Balidan Diwas of Guru Tegh Bahadur. The prominent issues raised across the country were opposition to divisive and violent politics and an end to the menace of terror in Kashmir—the central message being the superiority of India's unity above everything else. It was no surprise that the yatra received a rousing welcome across the country.

The success of the Ekta Yatra was a shot in the arm for the government at the Centre. It was also another significant milestone for Anandiben and other party workers. An emotional Anandiben watched the party's hard work bear fruit and her heart leapt with joy as the Tricolour finally fluttered against the Srinagar sky on 26 January 1992, hoisted by Modi and Joshi.

Anandiben, slowly and steadily, worked her way into the political system. She witnessed how Narendra Modi would handle people and situations. She learnt what it took to be in the system and how important it was to be a part of it to serve people. Once hesitant, she was later confident to take the next step.

On the personal front, Anandiben faced many challenges. Her son had ventured into some business that had not worked, but she did not use her political influence to empower her own family. She always believed that one should not misuse the nation's resources for personal gain. The other and more disruptive challenge was Mafatbhai, who had started disliking Anandiben's appraisal in the BJP. While he was sidelined, Anandiben was promoted for several party events. Mafatbhai started speaking against the party and his wife in public.

The third challenge was the school. Though Anandiben never compromised on her duties as the principal, the trustees did not like her political involvement. Trustee Mayaben started writing letters to Anandiben regarding the mismanagement of school affairs, even though there was no evidence to say there had been mismanagement, especially with Anandiben's personal involvement. Anandiben had not expected that these issues would arise, since she had continued to carry out all her duties with equal importance.

In 1995, with consistent efforts by Modi, Keshubhai Patel and other leaders like Anandiben, the BJP won 121 seats in the Gujarat Legislative Assembly elections and came to power with a majority. The party workers celebrated the first-ever victory with a majority of votes. This victory also gave India new hope, as it marked the BJP's arrival in mainstream politics. Gujarat was looking for a transformation and freedom from violence. Modi was praised profusely for his strategies and skills by party veterans such as Murli Manohar Joshi, Advani and Vajpayee. Keshubhai, who had organized the assembly election campaign, was appointed the chief minister of Gujarat on 14 March 1995. However, the tables turned sooner than expected.

When Anandiben was a Rajya Sabha Member of Parliament (MP), her husband was made panchayat vice president by the BJP and head of the education committee. In 1998, before the Gujarat Vidhan Sabha elections, Mafatbhai wrote two letters: one to Keshubhai Patel asking for a ticket for himself and another to Narendra Modi asking for a ticket for Anandiben. His intention behind this was that at least someone from the family would get a ticket to the elections.

BJP senior leader Suryakant Acharya, whose wife had served as a minister, suggested that Mafatbhai ask for a ticket for Anandiben as her chances of becoming a minister were stronger because of the hard work she had put in. Also, another reason, according to him, was the dearth of women leaders in the party. Acharya told Mafatbhai to have a big heart.

When a senior leader from the BJP, Dattaji Chirandas, asked Anandiben why she was not asking for a ticket, to which she innocently replied, 'I am a Rajya Sabha MP, how can an MP ask for a ticket?'

'But Mafatbhai is asking for a ticket for you,' he said.

Anandiben was surprised, but something else had been planned. Things got worse for Mafatbhai when Anandiben got a ticket from the Mandal constituency. That is when he started distributing pamphlets in protest against Anandiben. While everyone in the family supported Anandiben in her campaign, Mafatbhai did the opposite.

In 1998, Anandiben won from the Mandal constituency and became the education minister. In the next election, Mafatbhai campaigned against Anandiben, but she won in Patan too. This defeat was enough for Mafatbhai to stop interfering.

Road to Rajya Sabha

An eye for eye only ends up making the whole world blind.

—Mahatma Gandhi

As the BJP steadily ascended to the top, Anandiben, too, achieved a high point in 1995. She was nominated to become an MP in Rajya Sabha, the Upper House of Parliament, whose nominated members are picked by the president of India.

These MPs are luminaries from the world of economics, sports, literature, art, social service, and others. Anandiben had vast experience and knowledge in the field of education, social work, politics and sports. Though she was uncertain about her selection, Modi backed her nomination and encouraged her to take on the new responsibility.

Anandiben first went to Visnagar, to take the blessings of Saritaben before starting this new chapter in Parliament. All the teachers and students from her school were proud of her achievement and the journey she was embarking on. On the personal front, not everything was rosy: her husband was harbouring resentment. Anandiben did not let it deter her and, as always, decided to stay true to her purpose—working for the party and taking care of her children.

Anandiben became an MP. Everyone thought she was the most deserving candidate and that she symbolized hope for positive change. Anandiben herself was optimistic and ecstatic to be a part of Parliament. She had very limited knowledge of the sessions and her responsibilities, but leaders like Modi and Keshubhai guided her throughout. She had decided to work within the system and support the people of her country. She even took lessons to learn about Rajya Sabha and its sessions. She did not pause to celebrate the occasion; instead she planned for what was to come next and how to act.

Even amidst all the hustle and bustle of professional life, Anandiben never lost focus when it came to her children. She regularly discussed Shwetank's future plans with him. As long as she had to pay his college fee, she did not stop private tutoring after school. The finesse with which Anandiben managed her personal and professional life—both her political duties and her duties as a principal—did not come as a surprise to anyone, considering the grit and determination she had always shown. She would work for 20 hours a day at a stretch, making meals early in the morning, managing the school, visiting villages and organizing political events.

After becoming an MP, it was mandatory for her to attend sessions in Delhi. She was also given a house in the capital. Meanwhile, things started to get worse at Mohinaba. Mayaben started to create issues once Anandiben became an MP, even though, as per government policy, if a teacher becomes an MP, the management is bound to provide necessary leave for them to attend Rajya Sabha sessions. Meanwhile, Anandiben gave up her holidays to manage school work.

The political front wasn't resting easy either. In a few months, Gujarat faced its biggest political crisis. No one could have imagined that the newly elected BJP would split, just six months after coming to power. To everyone's shock, Shankersinh Vaghela revolted against Keshubhai Patel.

Modi had been the architect of the BJP's victory and a source of inspiration for many workers in the state. However, his consistent involvement in decision-making earned him the name 'Super Chief Minister'. Tension reigned within the party, and allegations of Modi's frequent intervention in government affairs led Keshubhai Patel to request the central leadership to shift Modi from Gujarat. On the other end, attending Rajya Sabha sessions in Delhi wasn't proving to be fulfilling enough for Anandiben. She had always wanted to work on the ground with people, so the sessions and the debates did not excite her much. She raised issues but her aim was to solve them while living in the society and not by sitting in a hall full of members.

Anandiben was also facing consistent issues with the trustees of Mohinaba during this time, who had by then indirectly asked her to resign. She was convinced about resigning but her lawyer suggested she fight for her rights. When Anandiben visited the school, she along with other teachers would wait for the notice. They started calling the notices *prem patras* as a joke. Everyone supported her because she did her job with full responsibility and had never let her Rajya Sabha sessions affect her work at the school.

She reviewed her decision to resign from the school and told the trustees that she won't be resigning until the issue of false notices and leave without pay (LWP) were resolved amicably.

Anandiben's life was never short on challenges. She shares another incident from this period in her life when her husband Mafatbhai went against the party. Shortly after Anandiben became the MP, Mafatbhai started writing articles against some BJP leaders. He was, at the time, the head of jila parishad. He was soon suspended from the party. He then joined Vaghela's team, who was planning a revolt against Modi and Keshubhai.

During an event, Anandiben came to know that Mafatbhai had published an article against the party which needed immediate attention. She called up Modi, who asked her to enquire about its publication. He asked Anandiben to inform Advani and join the party event. Anandiben was an honest person, so it did not come as a surprise to Advani that she was complaining about her husband, who was in the wrong. He asked her to be patient and continue doing the work. At the event, Anandiben was sitting on the stage with other dignitaries when she saw some people entering the venue and distributing pamphlets. The pamphlets eventually reached the guests sitting on stage.

'Who is doing all this?' an MP asked.

Anandiben looked away and read the pamphlet. 'This is my husband's doing,' she replied.

Narendra Modi asked her to leave the venue and reach the meeting centre. He then gathered everyone and told them about Anandiben's honesty and commitment to the party, and requested all party workers to not comment on the issue in public. The very next day, *Gujarat Samachar,* published the article with the headline, 'Anandiben's Husband Mafatbhai Speaks against BJP'. Anandiben called the media house and told them not to involve her. She was upset with the incident but she couldn't do much other than focus on her own work.

After the BJP had won majority in the Legislative Assembly, Modi backed Keshubhai Patel as the leader. Vaghela was not happy with the situation, and after Keshubhai was elected the new chief minister, support for Vaghela eventually waned.

Modi understood how the situation could pan out so he requested Keshubhai to conduct a party meeting to address all the brewing concerns. Instead, the Chief Minister left for a foreign trip and, in his absence, Vaghela rounded up 105 of 121 MLAs at his home in Vasan. As rebel MLAs flew out of the state, the state government collapsed. When Keshubhai resigned, the suggested names for the position of chief minister still did not include Vaghela. He revolted once again and, finally, broke the party in 1996.

The 11th Lok Sabha elections held in mid-1996 saw a hung parliament and a succession of three prime ministers within a span of two years. The country was forced into elections in 1998 again, and this time the BJP emerged as the only large party to win. However, the government formed by Atal Bihari Vajpayee folded after only 13 days in power.

In Gujarat, when Vaghela left the BJP with his supporters, he brought down the state government again. This time, he staked a claim to form the government with the support of the Congress under his newly formed political party, the Rashtriya Janata Party (RJP). But Vaghela's run as chief minister ended abruptly due to

Jethabhai Patel, father

Menaben Patel, mother

Anandiben with elder sister Saritaben's family

Anandiben with family members

Anandiben Patel with all her brothers and sisters

Anandiben Patel with her college degree

Anandiben Patel with Narendra Modi and Shankersinh Vaghela, 1989

Anandiben as part of Pilvai college team for state games, 1961

With BJP state leaders, 15 April 1991

Anandiben with Atal Bihari Vajpayee, former prime minister of India

Anandiben with L.K. Advani

Anandiben with senior leaders of the BJP

Narendra Modi welcomed at Ahmedabad station after Ekta Yatra, 31 January 1992

Mahila Morcha demonstration at Doordarshan, 30 December 1992

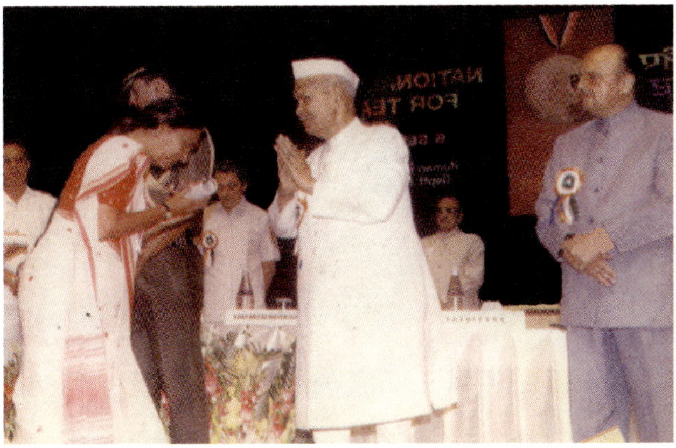

National Award for best teacher presented by Shankar Dayal Sharma, the then president of India, 1992

Welcome at Ahmedabad railway station after Ekta Yatra, 31 January 1992

After winning the Rajya Sabha election, 4 March 1994

Anandiben Patel honoured at the Dharti Vikas Mandal by L.K. Advani, 14 March 1994

Ananandiben Patel at the inaugration of a new broad gauge, Mehesana, Gujarat, 10 March 1996, as a Rajya Sabha member

Meeting Union Defence Minister George Fernandes with a delegation of Gujarat MPs, 1997

Anandiben Patel, Mridula Sinha and Keshubhai Patel at a women's rally, 6 January 1998

Oath-taking ceremony as Rajya Sabha member, 1998

Education minister Anandiben Patel at a meeting with L.K. Advani, the then deputy prime minister, Delhi, 1998

Vijay Rally after winning the election from Mandal district, January 1998

Ahmedabad Lokdarbar organized by the education department, 7 May 1999

Industrial seminar at Mandal Vidhan Sabha, 1999

Anandiben Patel attending an event as education minister

Bhuj earthquake relief work with Murli Mahohar Joshi, the then Union Human Resources Development Minister, 2001

Bhuj earthquake review meeting with L.K. Advani , 2001

Meeting students as education minister, 2001

School visit as education minister

Swearing in ceremony of the Narendra Modi Cabinet, 7 October 2001

Oath-taking ceremony as Cabinet Minister, 2002

Kanya Kelvni Yojna

At a Mahila Samelan meet

Bal Amrutam Yojna

Anandiben Patel with Amit Shah, the now minister of home affairs of India

the ongoing political turmoil. His fellow-rebel ex-BJP MLA Dilip Parikh was the next chief minister. Meanwhile, Modi had resigned from his position and written an article expressing his pledge that he would not allow Gujarat to be broken into pieces. The party realized Modi's intention and he was brought to Delhi and appointed as the general secretary. He was put in charge of the party's activities in Haryana and Himachal Pradesh. Anandiben was a witness to all this chaos.

That year, the trustees finally asked Anandiben to resign. She agreed, but put forward three conditions: to provide her the salaries due from false LWPs, to provide her house rent allowance (HRA) and to take back all the notices against her. She was honest and knew that she hadn't done anything wrong. It was only when the trustees accepted all her conditions that Anandiben resigned from Mohinaba Vidyalaya. It was a shock for the staff and students, but no one could do anything to stop her. Anandiben had tried her best to manage the situation but things had gotten worse for her at both ends. Her best friend and colleague, Meenakshiben, was elected as the next principal of Mohinaba Kanya Vidyalaya.

Mirroring the political instability at the Centre, fresh elections for Gujarat had to be called in 1998. Modi suggested Anandiben's name for a ticket in the 1998 general elections. Anandiben was now working full-time for the party, and people had been witnessing her grit and strength for a decade now, but she was not sure of contesting elections. There were talks of giving her the ticket to contest from Sarkhej but later it was given to Amit Shah and she was given the Mandal constituency, which was a tough seat to crack.

When she had gotten the offer to become Rajya Sabha MP in 1994, she had said no because her children had been young. She had been giving tuitions and working at the school and had cited these as reasons for not being ready to take on bigger opportunities. For her, her children and running her home were her priority. But now, Modi called her and said, 'You should not say no to opportunities. You have worked so hard for years, now is the time to make a bigger impact. The party will not give someone so many chances.' That is when she decided to take the opportunity.

In the Vidhan Sabha elections, she did not ask for a ticket. The party thought that women should be made to contest and they knew there was no better option than her. Even though she knew it would be difficult for a Patel to win from Mandal, she said yes to the ticket and attempted her best. She says, '*Haarne ke liye bhi ladna toh padhega naa* (In order to lose, we will have to contest, right)?'

A hesitant Anandiben said 'yes' to the elections and people all around her questioned her decision. Her husband went so far as to tell the family members that she had no chance of winning. Anandiben did not listen to anyone. For her, it was important to try. She had never given up anything in life because of the fear of failure. She wanted to serve the country and she knew if she won the election, she would be able to work for the people in a more effective manner. She just remembered the words of her father, 'Never give up, daughter', and her path was clear in front of her.

Modi's encouragement played a significant role in Anandiben's life. She knew Modi was a visionary and that if he had suggested her name, he must trust her and her capabilities. But there were now groups within the party, and people who supported Modi were given tough seats, setting them up for failure and in an attempt at tarnishing Modi's reputation.

As soon as Anandiben's name was announced for the Mandal constituency, the Patel division started preparing for her campaign.

'She will lose by 10,000 votes,' Mafatbhai laughed while having dinner with the family.

Shwetank and Anar encouraged Anandiben to ignore their father. The children had been supportive from the very beginning of Anandiben's political journey. They had issues, they faced troubles, but they knew that it was all for a greater good. They understood Anandiben's purpose and vision. While she silently cared for them and nurtured them to grow into human beings with strong principles, they created a strong family bond. With Mafatbhai supporting the Congress, Anandiben started her campaign in Mandal.

In the 1998 Lok Sabha and assembly elections of Gujarat, Modi focused on nominating candidates who were familiar with the ground reality and were connected to the people at the grassroots. His aim was to get educated and hard-working people to win the elections. He supported the MLAs who stayed with the party during the time of the crisis.

In New Delhi, Modi's equation with senior leaders was going through a transformation. He formed a great relationship with Murli Manohar Joshi, Advani and Vajpayee. He was put in charge of the 1998–99 elections and returned to Gujarat to appeal to the voters to support the party. He was not very fond of Keshubhai's leadership. Some people considered Keshubhai an arrogant leader, but he had the full support of the Patel community.

When Anandiben reached Mandal, people recognized her, and she was greeted warmly because of her selfless work during the bird flu epidemic. It almost seemed like she was a Bollywood star, and the people her fans—people had kept track of the work she had been doing. Anar and Shwetank formed different teams to visit the villages. They would carry out surveys, talk to people about their issues and make status reports. Due to her notable work with the Dharti Vikas Mandal, she garnered unstinted support across all the villages.

She was also called by the Meghmani family, who held great influence over Mandal's voters. She was welcomed and told that people admired her work. People wanted someone who was educated and worked for society irrespective of the candidate's caste and region. People wanted to elect someone who would work for them, and this was Modi's vision. She got massive support from the voters. People knew that Anandiben had the potential to become a minister, and that she would transform the district with the state. People wilfully offered donations for her campaign. Villagers offered meals and shelter to her team. She was so happy to see the love people were showering on her. She wanted to give back all the love and support. She went door to door and met people. She visited schools, anganwadis and NGOs. She continued motivating people to get their daughters educated.

But if she was loved and respected by thousands of people, there was a section of people who would go to any lengths to malign her, especially during elections. This time, right before the elections, a local journalist from Patan wrote an article regarding Anandiben owning a bungalow worth ₹5 crore. This went on for some time, with the same journalist constantly increasing the amount in each article he wrote. Sometimes the ₹5 crores became ₹50 crores, sometimes, some other figure. She wanted to file a case against the newspaper.

She took permission from Modiji and filed a case, which she won. The High Court banned the newspaper for spreading fake news. The local press was also shut, but, considering the fact that many people would lose their jobs if the press shut down, Anandiben went to court after six months and requested the reopening of the press. This was her attitude towards those wanting to pull her down.

As election day approached, thousands of voters gathered at polling stations across the villages. Anandiben was standing against Jayantibhai Patel of the Congress, who already had a strong political hold in the constituency. Everyone in Anandiben's family was nervous. She visited her home in Kharod and later received Saritaben's blessings in Visnagar as well.

'No matter whether you win or lose, people admire your good work. That is what matters in the end,' Saritaben said as the day of the results approached.

The counting of votes in Gujarat's assembly election showed the BJP leading in most of the constituencies. Modi won from Rajkot and Anandiben from Mandal with a margin of 5,000 votes, getting a total of 32,000 votes against Jayantibhai's 27,000.

There was immense joy and excitement among the supporters. Anandiben felt confident and strong. She now had a clear vision: to assist the people of her constituency. From the moment she won the election, she started making plans for the villages. Reaching such a stage in her life had not been easy for Anandiben. It was a result of her own struggle for education, her fight against regressive societal norms and rituals, her hard work as a teacher and her commitment as a party worker. From sleepless nights to constantly being on the move during the day from village to village to campaign in the hot sun, it was all leading to a bright future for the state. The journey of a leader had begun; the roar of Gujarat's lioness reverberating across the state.

Anandiben's supporters organized a road show in Mandal. With the crowd chanting *'Lamba Jivanta, Anandiben* (Long live, Anandiben)', she held a march in her constituency to express her gratitude. Accompanied by her children and party workers, she met local people and thanked them for bestowing their trust upon her. People gathered in large numbers and raised the party flag.

Modi congratulated Anandiben on her victory and told her to keep doing the good work. In the state, the BJP returned to power with Keshubhai at the helm again on March 1998. Vaghela finally merged his party with the Congress and didn't contest elections.

Anandiben assumed office the same day, while the other winners continued to celebrate. She sometimes felt all alone, but after receiving so much love from the people, she made 'serving people' her life's goal. Work would give her all the happiness she needed.

Anandiben has always believed in politics where people support each other. Politicians make strategies to remain in power, but she focused on giving her best effort in order to secure the welfare of her constituents. She often reminisces about the support she received from her male colleagues—they were all just that, colleagues, gender never played a role in their equations. It was always a collaborative effort, she supported her ministers and they, in turn, supported her.

Anandiben was the first woman to be given charge of the Revenue, Public Works, Urban Housing, etc. She remembers that when she held the majority of the departments, she would call other departments proactively and ask them to share their requirements and inputs. She always kept a straight face and ensured that discipline was maintained.

Her modus operandi always was working at the grassroots and trying to resolve the smallest of issues. She started from the smaller issues and worked her way up. She worked on water problems, roads, education and child marriage. She made it an inclusive constituency where everyone was treated as equals. Carrying Jethabhai's values, she worked against backward rituals. Following the steps of Daulatbhai, she transformed the education system in the villages. And finally, keeping Modi's vision in mind, she worked with full honesty and commitment. She personally supported the people who approached her for help. She paid the school fees for underprivileged children and contributed to fulfilling the critical medical needs of families. As Anandiben says, 'People who work honestly face more challenges but in the end the truth prevails.'

As time passed, the central leadership noted that Keshubhai was involved in dwindling industrial investments and inactive development, and there were also complaints of abuse of power which led to demands for his removal. When the search for a new leader to head the government began, the central leaders were not concerned about the successor's caste profile, or Keshubhai's potential to create trouble. During his last few interactions with the central leaders in Delhi, Keshubhai had even threatened to quit the party if he was not allowed to have a say in the choice of his successor. But the party turned down his suggestion that one of its Union Ministers from Gujarat be sent to Gandhinagar, on the grounds that it would lead to two by-elections, one to the assembly and the other to the Lok Sabha. The central leaders were convinced that Keshubhai Patel had squandered his mandate of 1998 and no one of his choice would be able to stop the party's slide in the state. Thus, Modi, who had remained unmatched as the leader of the party and government in the state, became their choice.

There are several snippets of information regarding Anandiben that indicate how she is as a person: selfless, determined, self-respecting and firm in her beliefs. She recalls an episode where a mother had brought her daughter, who was 18 at the time, saying that no one was willing to marry her since her lip was cut from the middle. Anandiben asked her team if something could be done about it and as per suggestion, the girl underwent plastic surgery. Anandiben, since then, has given the go-ahead for 10,000 children to undergo plastic surgery. She has always been a patient listener and done everything in her capacity to solve any problem and has never turned away someone in need, such has been her drive to help people.

She learnt from the people who came to her for help and introduced schemes in order to help other people going through the same thing. For example, the Mukhyamantri Amrutam (MA) Yojana and the MA Vatsalya Yojana provide tertiary care treatment to the below poverty line (BPL) population and to the families with an annual income of ₹2.50 lakh or below ₹2.50 lakh per annum. All beneficiaries can avail cashless quality medical and surgical treatment for illnesses that are catastrophic. This scheme was created for people who had no BPL cards and could not make ends meet. Anandiben has always found ways to uplift the people, and she has stood like a rock for her children, her fellow party members, her party and her state.

Minister of Education

What is really needed to make democracy function is not knowledge of facts but right education.

—Mahatma Gandhi

Anandiben represented India in the fourth World Women's Conference held in Beijing, China, with Bhavna Chikhalia, who was the then executive secretary and vice president of the BJP in Gujarat. She also accompanied Vajpayee and P.A. Sangma, Speaker of the Lok Sabha, to Bulgaria, before resigning as MP.

The 12th Lok Sabha elections in 1998 did not provide the country with a stable government. Even though Vajpayee took oath as the 16th prime minister of India, the government only lasted for 13 months. Once the All India Anna Dravida Munnetra Kazhagam (AIADMK) withdrew its support, the party did not garner any further numbers. After that, the then president of India, K.R. Narayanan, turned to the leader of the Opposition in Lok

Sabha, Sonia Gandhi, to form the government. When she responded with the United Progressive Alliance 's (UPA) inability to form the government, the president dissolved the House.

The 13th Lok Sabha elections held in 1999, fortunately, provided the country with a stable government that lasted for five years. The majority group in the Lok Sabha during this period was the National Democratic Alliance (NDA), a Centre-Right group led by the BJP, which won 270 seats, 16 more than the last election. The NDA, under the leadership of Vajpayee, completed a full term until the next general elections—the first non-Congress government to do so.

The scenario in Gujarat, however, was still volatile. Keshubhai's government was being increasingly unpredictable. Meanwhile, Anandiben had become the minister for education in Keshubhai's Cabinet, where Bharat Barot had been given the department for higher education. Anandiben had also been given the additional charge of women and child development.

Anandiben's joy and satisfaction now knew no bounds. She finally had the means to do everything that was needed to transform the education system of the state and create a replicable model for the entire country.

This was also the time when Gujarat was going through a crisis in its education system. There had been no proper recruitments in the last 10 years. Schools lacked basic facilities like toilets and proper drinking water. In addition, the high school dropout rate was restricting the progress of education in the state. At the time of Anandiben's taking charge of the education ministry, people were quite angry at the condition of the schools. This was going to be another big challenge but she was determined to overcome it.

When Anandiben assumed office, she first took time to comprehensively understand the processes. The officers would come to her just to take her signatures or with transfer requests. She understood that things had been run in such a perfunctory way for years that now it was time to bring about a change. She took on board the policies, budgets and organizational operations, and prepared a task list.

The most important and urgent task at hand was the recruitment of teachers. There were reports of corruption in the recruitment process and many cases had been filed too. Anandiben started the Vidya Sahayak Yojana, a campaign with an aim to transparently recruit teachers on the basis of merit to fill positions that had been lying vacant in government schools for the past 10 years. It was for the first time that the state was witnessing a government ministry that worked transparently. There were no bribes or recommendations involved in the process. With the help of this scheme, more than one lakh teachers were recruited in government schools. With this first step as the education minister, Anandiben had won the hearts of the people.

She also visited schools across the state and noted down the flaws in their facilities. Her vast experience as a teacher and as a principal stood her in good stead throughout her tenure. The trustees, who were against her before, invited her now to be the chief guest at the Mohinaba Kanya Vidyalaya.

The next major challenge was the issue of teacher transfers. Anandiben decided to transfer the teachers on the basis of their experience and age. She established residential quarters for junior teachers to encourage taking up transferable posts. She was credited for her work in reducing corruption in the teacher-transfer processes.

An incident during these overhauls is clearly etched in Anandiben's mind. Once when she made a surprise visit to a Buniyadi Shiksha Vidyalaya (primary schools based on Gandhiji's principles; there were 200 such schools in Gujarat, managed by a trust that gets 100 per cent of its funding from government grants), she found that the examination papers had not been checked properly, for example, students who had not written anything in their answer sheets were given 80 marks. She promptly called the teachers to provide a justification. On receiving no reasonable answers, she asked the officer-in-charge to collect all the papers and send them back for rechecking, and gave them a week to finish the task. Proper rechecking showed very bad results and low pass percentages for the entire chain of schools in that district.

This incident riled the school trustees up and they went to Modi to complain against Anandiben. On the other end, Anandiben, too, had called up Modi to report the incident. She did not know then that he had already scheduled a meeting with the trustees. He, too, didn't mention it and instead asked for the answer sheets from her.

In the meeting, all the district education officers and Congress MLAs were present. They explained the situation to Modi, citing Anandiben's interference as the problem. They stated how the bad results would tarnish the image and reputation of the school.

Modi asked his officer to distribute those very answer sheets to everyone in the meeting and asked, 'What should we do about this?'

Everyone looked down. There was pin-drop silence in the room.

Modi took a long look at them and began, 'This has been

happening for years. Our objective is to educate people. Why can't we teach the children well and get them to get decent marks rather than going the other way? How will this take our state forward? I thank Anandiben for doing this. Now tell me, how do you want to work?'

The trustees accepted their mistake and went back to work without further questions.

If it seems like Modi trusts every action and decision taken by Anandiben, it is because she has never failed him. He knew that she joined politics with the intention of serving the people and that is what he always counted on.

In 2000, teachers went on a huge strike. Anandiben had more or less anticipated this move before the next elections. The teachers threatened to derail conducting examinations, a move that would severely affect the children's future. These strikes, timed just before the elections, were used to get their demands fulfilled by the government, which would bow down in fear of losing the elections.

The point of contention was Anandiben's declaration that made the recruitment of teachers dependent solely on merit and qualifications. The elimination of interviews in the recruitment process left no room for corrupt practices such as recommendations, and introduced transparency—the primary reason for the strike.

Many ministers and other leaders within the party also opposed her but she did not get swayed. She reminded them that they had fought the election with an agenda to eradicate 'fear, hunger and corruption', and she meant to stick to it. She was firm in her actions and knew that it would later act as a support system for the collapsing education system in Gujarat. Anandiben's crusade continued and she visited many teacher recruitment centres. She promptly invalidated any recruitment camp where she saw corruption.

The strike continued.The teachers now wanted a common solution to all their many problems. Anandiben decided to face this challenge as well. She personally met the teachers and listened to the problems they were facing. She reassured them that she was dedicatedly and directly working on several issues, such as their transfers, recruitments and also improving the conditions of the schools. There were more than five lakh teachers who were still on strike.

At this stage, Anandiben declared an emergency in the ministry. She told the teachers to get back to work or else risk a break in their service. She started recruiting more teachers and announced a campaign stating: 'No Work, No Pay'. The teachers threatened to collapse the government but Anandiben remained unfazed.

She stood for what was right; she was not at all bothered that she could lose in the next elections for the stand she had taken. This adherence to the true path and zeal for change made her position stronger. She tried to show the teachers that the growth and development of the state were in their hands. She asked them, 'If the children see you going on strikes for no apparent reason, what will they learn?' Anandiben led by example. It was clear to everyone that she practised what she preached. It was a rare virtue in an individual, let alone a politician, and this inspired trust.

After 18 days of struggle, the strike ended. Since that day, there have been no strikes by the teachers of the state. A few months later, both the party and the teachers saw a drastic improvement in the education system. Schools were in much better condition, the results of many schools improved, and deserving teachers found their place in the classrooms. Anandiben knew that it is always tough to bring about change at first, but once initiated, it flows positively on its own.

Anandiben then trained her focus on the primary schools and anganwadis. She knew that the foundation of education in children was really important. Apart from the infrastructure, she also worked on the curriculum and teaching methods. She regularly held meetings with the trustees of different schools and discussed the possibilities of improving the education structure. She started another statewide campaign in relation to it called the Pravesh Utsav-Kanya Kelvani Mahotsav to encourage the enrolment of more and more students in schools, especially girls.

From the chief minister to the MPs, everyone joined the festival of education. All the officers at the district level promoted this campaign for education. From cities to villages, the idea was a huge success. The process of getting admission and studying in government schools saw a sea change. Schools were decorated and children celebrated with their parents. The former students were given awards, cultural events were organized and toppers were felicitated by the trustees.

Anandiben's efforts resulted in a 100 per cent increase in enrolment. The school dropout rate came down too. Anandiben also established a school for disabled children. Not only children, but their families were also involved with the school management. The state witnessed a step towards a complete overhaul of its education system because of her vast experience in the field. This campaign ultimately became the inspiration for the very well-known 'Beti Bachao, Beti Padhao' campaign that focuses on the prevention of female foeticide and promotion of girl child education, reaffirming the mark of a true leader and educationist: Anandiben Patel.

'Shala Praveshotsav' is still the flagship programme of the education department in Gujarat. In her first term as education minister, Anandiben also started 'Lok Darbar' to address issues related to schools and education. It was under her leadership that the system became a platform for people to come forward and participate.

Apart from education, Anandiben knew that there were many other challenges that women faced. She had a close understanding of how women were not completely free from traditional customs, community rituals and orthodox social regulations. She had been brought up by her parents to always stand against such unhealthy practices and continued to encourage others to do so as well. Whenever other women needed her support, she met them and counselled their families.

In 1998, Anandiben was working as the representative of the Mandal constituency. It was a common perception among the people that after winning the elections, a candidate moves on to 'bigger' things, forgetting about the constituency they had stood from and the promises they had made to the people of that constituency to better their lot, and to garner votes, of course. Anandiben, in contrast, religiously visited the villages of Mandal after winning. Most of the areas there belonged to the Rajput community. She started building a strong relationship with the villagers. She failed to elicit a response initially but did not leave the issues unaddressed.

Anandiben always tried to engage women and understand their problems. She observed that during gatherings, political and otherwise, a section of women in her constituency would participate in dark-coloured sarees, looking poor and neglected. This group of women, she further came to know, subsisted on the fringes of society. They were almost boycotted by society. Upon asking around, she came to know that they were widows who had been shunned by society. Their condition was intolerable for Anandiben. She wanted to improve their plight and create social awareness in the village.

She initiated a pension scheme for widows and asked her colleagues, Paragbhai and Sureshbhai, to lead other voluntary workers in the village to fill in application forms and procure other documents from these women. The scheme was implemented with the cooperation of the administration. She opted for a simpler process where women availing benefits from the pension scheme were not asked to visit the offices, rather the officials visited the village.

After the scheme was implemented, the women personally thanked Anandiben. The task was a small one, but it was the first time that these women were moved from the periphery and brought into focus. Anandiben's values and experience played an important role in this, especially the inspiration she had received from Jethabhai and Saritaben, who always stood for the betterment of widows. She still remembered the incidents following her sister Saritaben's widowhood and the challenges she had had to face. Anandiben's purpose was to make women self-reliant and empowered through education as well as upliftment schemes.

During her tenure at Mandal, she transformed the entire constituency. From establishing new schools to creating flexible processes for the villagers, she changed the face of Mandal. Her work was praised not only in the constituency but in the entire state. Modi, in particular, was really impressed with his apprentice.

All these achievements were not without their own challenges, that too from leaders within the party. Anandiben recalls locking horns with Haren Pandya, who represented the Ellis Bridge constituency of Ahmedabad for the BJP. When Keshubhai became the chief minister of Gujarat in 1998, Pandya, who was his strongest supporter, was inducted into the state Cabinet as the minister of home affairs. Later, when Modi took charge as the chief minister in 2001, Pandya was moved to the post of minister of state for revenue. He resigned in August 2002.

There were many incidents where Haren Pandya interrupted Anandiben and interfered with her work. He would call for meetings and fail to appear while she waited for him having left her own work, keep approvals pending, etc. This behaviour disturbed Anandiben's focus and derailed her projects. Pandya often indirectly opposed the policies and decisions that Anandiben pushed in the education department. Finally, she confronted him one day and asked him to become the education minister instead and offered to resign. After this, Pandya stopped sticking his nose where it did not belong.

All this while, Anandiben's conjugal life remained unstable. The conflicts with Mafatbhai increased every day. The spats stemmed from his obvious dissatisfaction with his position in politics vis-à-vis Anandiben's. Their children, however, brought some joy to her life and offered her contentment.

Her daughter, Anar, had married Jayesh Patel, son of renowned social worker Ishwar Patel, who was famously known as the 'Toilet

Man of India'. Shwetank, Anandiben's son, had established his IT business and printing press, and gotten married to a homely woman, Hina. Both the children had had a low-key wedding ceremony. They believed that since Anandiben had struggled a lot to pay for their education, the burden of arranging for their marriages and related events should not fall on her shoulders, as no other financial support was forthcoming. Such were the values they possessed.

A year passed by thus. Anandiben proved her worth and staunchness towards the welfare of society in her professional capacity. On the personal front, she dealt with her circumstances in the best way possible and took solace in the little things that worked out right.

It was Republic Day in 2001, and Anandiben was in the city of Godhra to unfurl the national flag. As she entered the school campus and was about to take her seat inside, the entire campus ground began to tremble. Everyone looked around unsettled as the floor and the whole room continued to shake.

'It's an earthquake!' a teacher screamed and took all the students to the playground.

Anandiben instructed everyone to move to a safe open space and vacate the school premises. The students were scared and ran for open ground. The tremors went on for the next few seconds, but there was no damage to the premises. Anandiben made sure that all the attendees and children were safe. She then went and inspected the nearby areas and returned to Ahmedabad.

The commercial hub of Gujarat was in a state of panic. Many high-rise buildings had toppled, and several were feared dead. She could see people running helter-skelter, trying to locate friends and family, arranging medical help for the injured or crying for their loved ones who had died. Children were marching on the streets as it was Republic Day and a lot of them were buried under the debris of the buildings.

The 2001 Bhuj earthquake, as it would be called in the future, was of 7.7 magnitude on the Mw (moment magnitude) scale with its epicentre in Bhachau Taluka of Kutch. It destroyed a huge area, flattening cities including the district capital Bhuj, and wrecking over 8,000 villages. The entire nation was in shock. This was the most challenging time for the government of Gujarat. Anandiben went back to her office and asked her officials to prepare a list of affected schools and shelter homes.

The phones in her office rang incessantly. It was a challenge for her to respond to everything at the same time. The most important thing for her was to ensure the health of the children. She wanted to make sure that the children emerged unscathed from the disaster. After that, she shifted her focus and responsibility to ensure that they had all the supplies and facilities. She immediately took the decision to close the school down.

There was considerable damage to life and property in many areas. Thousands of people had lost their lives and many houses had collapsed. More than a million became homeless. The areas hit majorly were Kutch and Saurashtra.

Anandiben began by working towards reducing panic and fear in the state. With this aim, she decided to reopen the schools and keep them working, even in the affected areas, to distract children from the disaster. Many school buildings had collapsed too. Reconstructing these structures was an uphill task.

She had tents and food arranged for the children. The officials distributed books, pens and other material among the children. Anandiben visited different districts and inspected the buildings to check if they could still host board exams. After her scrutiny, it was decided to hold examinations in April and then again in June for the children who had been injured in the earthquake. Such students were kept in a special category. She did not want them to feel pressured about exams after the tragic event.

Anandiben also visited the hospitals to meet the injured. She interacted with many injured children and observed their conditions. She motivated them to pull through the adverse circumstances. Many children bravely shared their stories and were happy to see her. She particularly remembers meeting a boy who was pulled out of the debris after seven days. She asked him how he had survived.

'I drank my own urine,' the little boy replied.

Tears gathered in Anandiben's eyes as she patted his back, 'You are a brave boy!'

It was a tough time for the people of Gujarat and leaders like Anandiben chose to be with the people. Her constant visits and meetings with the children motivated them throughout the unfortunate times.

On Modi's advice, she met the then home minister, Murli Manohar Joshi, and visited the length and breadth of the affected areas. They observed that many colleges and school buildings had been damaged. The home ministry immediately offered monetary aid of ₹150 crore to the education ministry in Gujarat. Engineers were hired to create a survey report and a plan of action. Several committees were formed to offer financial support to the victims. Within a few months, the education system was up and running.

Anandiben had wept with the parents whose children had been affected by this tragedy and vowed to support them in every possible way. She started the 'Vidhyadeep Yojana' scheme during this time. It was launched to provide round-the-clock insurance and financial assistance to students studying in government primary schools, grant-in-aid primary schools, ashram schools and secondary- and higher-secondary schools. The premium for this scheme is paid by the government. The guardian is paid an amount upon the death of his child. The families suffering from an incomparable loss were offered yearly compensation under this scheme.

The death toll in the affected region reached around 20,000 people, while the estimate for the injured was pegged at 150,000. The Bhuj earthquake destroyed properties worth crores of rupees, including residential and public structures and historic sites, and also damaged water bodies and local crops. While the Indian military carried out rescue-and-support operations, financial aid and supplies poured in from many countries and international organizations.

The Gujarat Earthquake Reconstruction and Rehabilitation Policy was announced after a gap of four months by the state government. The policy was aimed at rebuilding physical and social infrastructure, economic revival, health support and community reconstruction. However, the handling of the 2001 earthquake by the state administration under Keshubhai Patel left much to be desired. There were many rumours and allegations about corruption and misuse of power. The loss of a few by-elections in state assembly seats and Keshubhai's failing health flagged-off the search for a new head of the state.

The BJP national leadership now sought a new candidate for the post of chief minister. Senior BJP leaders like Advani were not inclined to ostracize Patel and were concerned about Modi's lack of experience in government. Modi, who had expressed misgivings about Patel's administration, declined the offer of deputy chief minister under Patel. Some sources have said that he told Advani and Vajpayee that he was either going to be fully responsible for Gujarat or not at all.

On 3 October 2001, Modi replaced Keshubhai as the chief minister of Gujarat, with the responsibility of preparing the BJP for the December 2002 elections.

In keeping with this aim, Anandiben was transferred from Mandal to Patan constituency. The BJP wanted to establish a stronghold in north Gujarat, where a majority of the population was from the Patidar community, and Anandiben Patel became the obvious and deserving choice to lay this foundation. She was educated and respected for her work as a minister and a woman with a strong vision whom people looked up to.

She had faced some resistance in Patan during the teachers' strike, while people from the Mandal constituency had selflessly supported her. If there were 10 people who opposed her, a 10,000-strong crowd stood by her. She got massive support from people who had benefited from her actions in the education, and women and child development (WCD) departments.

Modi was sworn in as the chief minister on 7 October 2001, and entered the Gujarat state legislature on 24 February 2002 by winning a by-election to the Rajkot II constituency, defeating the Congress's Ashwin Mehta. On the other hand, Anandiben won the Patan constituency after defeating Kantilal Patel. Her portfolio of impressive work as the education and WCD minister garnered her more than 50,000 votes.

That year, a shocking and tragic incident took over Gujarat. The Sabarmati Express train filled with Hindu pilgrims returning to Gujarat from Ayodhya halted at Godhra. The area had a dominant 40 per cent Muslim population. The pilgrims were chanting religious slogans inside the train when the coach was set on fire, burning 58 Hindu pilgrims alive. This barbaric incident became the cause of a three-day communal riot. The next day, the VHP called for a strike across the state. However, anti-Muslim violence spread throughout Gujarat and soon, cities, towns and villages started feeling the heat of rioting and arson.

Modi, who had only been in power a few months, endorsed peace and prosperity. He directed a massive paramilitary force deployment on the same day and the army was marching the streets within 48 hours, on 1 March 2002.

The total number of deaths reached 1,044 of which 790 were Muslims and the rest, Hindus.[1] Hundreds were still missing and

[1] 'Gujarat Riot Death Toll Revealed', BBC, 11 May 2005, https://bbc.in/3Q9xOZB. Accessed on 9 August 2022.

several thousand homes and businesses, and hundreds of places of worship had been destroyed. The riots displaced roughly 150,000 people statewide.[2]

Anandiben visited many refugee camps and hospitals to meet the injured. She was especially concerned about the children and worked towards providing official and personal support to the ones affected by the massacres. Although curfew was imposed in 26 major cities, the authorities were unable to prevent violence from escalating in many pockets.

In the aftermath of the violence, the education of children was severely disrupted. Certificates and other documents of many children had been destroyed, and schoolgoing students were still facing threats of attack. Anandiben, being the education minister of the state, intervened in the matter. Her first decision was to postpone the annual board exams from March to April, since she knew the riots had left a deep impact on many families.

Her next challenge was to ensure the safety of Muslim students. She called an emergency meeting of her department one morning.

'Madam, we received a notification that two MLAs have announced that Muslim students won't give exams,' a senior officer said as the meeting started.

'I will speak to the MLAs. I need a comprehensive list of all Muslim schools,' Anandiben directed in a firm voice. 'We need to provide security to the students. I will personally go and meet the parents to assure them of their children's safety. We can't let students suffer because of all this.'

---

[2]Rubin, Oliver, *Democracy and Famine*, Routledge, 2010, pp. 172–73.

That same day, Anandiben with her officers went to affected areas like Shakarpur and Akbarpur in Khambat. A few senior leaders warned her against visiting the place but she did not listen. She had decided to meet the parents and children in the affected areas, and she wasn't going to backtrack at this point.

The town was still disturbed after the communal clashes. The old coastal area looked like a ghost town with toppled cars, destroyed markets and burnt homes. In the midst of a curfew, Anandiben called out to the Muslim families. The community gathered around her, outside.

'We have postponed exams in many areas like Ahmedabad, Vadodara, Bharuch and Modasa. We don't want our children to compromise with their education. We will provide buses and police security for your children to reach the examination centres safely and we will be recording the entire day. You don't have to worry. We are with you,' Anandiben assured them. She also spoke to the parents individually and asked about the requirements of their children. Her visit made a lot of difference to the people.

When Vajpayee called Anandiben after an argument had ensued in Rajya Sabha over Muslim students not being able to give exams in Gujarat, she presented the data which showed that the number of Muslim students who had appeared for the exam the same year was higher than the previous year. He was impressed by her efforts.

Anandiben was concerned about the situation in Gujarat University, where exams had been disrupted by angry mobs. Rioters had even threatened Muslim students to deter them from attending examinations. Anandiben arranged for police vans to be stationed in all these sensitive areas in order to help with the smooth conduct of the exams that all the students in schools and universities were to sit for. Her efforts paid off and lakhs of Muslim students concluded their examinations successfully. Anandiben's initiatives were praised in the community and a felicitation event was organized in her honour.

To this, Anandiben politely responded, 'I could not have done all this without the support of Modiji. You should call him for the event.'

'But we are Muslims. Will he come?' the organizers from the community asked.

'Why won't he? These are all misconceptions about him made up by people who are doing politics with the situation. Modiji considers everyone equal. Of course, he will come,' Anandiben explained calmly.

Two days later, Modi attended the programme and met the affected children. He asked them about their examinations and other problems they faced. In Lok Sabha, Anandiben confidently announced that the riots had not lowered the percentage of students sitting for exams. She was highly praised for her willpower and efforts.

By March 2002, nearly 150,000 displaced people had moved into relief camps, roughly numbering 104.[3] These camps were run by community groups and NGOs, with support from the government in the form of amenities and supplementary services.

For the upcoming elections, the BJP's campaign was to be led by Chief Minister Modi. However, he was largely being targeted and accused by human rights groups of deliberately failing to

---

[3]Ibid.

protect Muslims during the rioting. It was a false charge that the BJP denied.

In the aftermath of the violence, widespread voices within and outside the state asked Modi to resign. Although Vajpayee, the then prime minister of India, did not dismiss Modi for his handling of the riots, opposition parties stalled Parliament over the issue. Modi submitted his resignation at the April 2002 BJP national executive meeting in Goa, but it was not accepted. Thereafter, his Cabinet held an emergency meeting on 19 July 2002, after which he offered his resignation again to the governor of Gujarat, S.S. Bhandari, and the State Assembly was dissolved.

The BJP called for early elections and Modi won a landslide victory which was a referendum on his brand of politics. The party had been governing Gujarat since 1998 and was also heading the coalition government at the Centre. The BJP won 127 seats in the 182-member assembly and silenced all the critics and naysayers. Modi won the Maninagar constituency while Anandiben retained her seat in Patan constituency, along with the charge of the education ministry and the WCD department.

Like always, Shwetank and Anar stood by her and supported her election campaign. In contrast, her relationship with Mafatbhai showed no signs of improvement on account of his bitterness. He had actually never imagined that Anandiben would be promoted to the highest rungs of the party. He neither believed in her noble character nor recognized her efforts to support the family along with the party. Nonetheless, Anandiben moved on against all the odds and fears, with an aim to work for her nation and serve its people with integrity.

During her second stint, women made up around 50 per cent of the population of Gujarat and about 25 per cent were children. As the head of the WCD department, it was a big responsibility for Anandiben to protect and nurture them. From education to security, she worked on all the minute aspects. The WCD department existed on paper but until Anandiben assumed office, there had been no work done on the ground. There was no grant, no staff and no set processes in the department.

The WCD department was established within 15 days of Modi taking charge as the chief minister for the first time. Anandiben created welfare schemes for women and children from the ground up. She focused first on the health and education of children from backward areas. She strengthened livelihood schemes for women. Anandiben started self-help groups, opened bank accounts, assigned ration cards and introduced women's stake in family property. She believed that the country flourished only if its women were empowered.

Anandiben completely modernized and remodelled the anganwadis with the support of Modi. She believed that the foundation of children needed to be strong and effective. Prior to her charge, many anganwadis were functioning under NGOs and other government organizations. She appointed new staff members and teachers, and created dedicated infrastructure. She then categorized and mapped them to different schools. Most anganwadis were previously operating outside homes or government offices.

Major support came from Modi, who backed the revitalization of the WCD department by authorizing state government grants. Within a few months, a new image of anganwadis was established in

Gujarat. The new versions provided toilets, midday meals and other facilities. The curriculum for anganwadis was created by educationists. As encouragement, Anandiben also started the 'Mata Yashoda' Award for anganwadi teachers. The role of the worker and helper at the anganwadi level is very important in the operation of the integrated child development scheme. In order to provide incentives to the anganwadi workers and helpers of the state, incentive awards are given at the state, district, corporation and project level.

Anandiben often undertook surprise visits to schools, spoke to the children, and talked about the challenges and problems they faced. She observed the teaching methods and advised adopting activity-based learning, which she had learnt from Daulatbhai Desai. She ordered schools to organize tours and exhibitions to encourage exposure to the outside world.

Continuing her inspirational work in education, Anandiben started focusing on the health of children. During her school visits, she witnessed that many children in the state were suffering from various health issues which remained neglected due to a lack of awareness and funds. She knew something had to be done because education could only do so much if the child was unhealthy. Besides, these children would be unable to participate in sports. She issued an advisory for the school management systems to organize health check-up camps and share survey reports with the local authorities. She launched the 'School Health Programme' drive across the state. The campaign was started in collaboration with leading doctors who would visit the schools and inspect the health of students. The government supported all the expenses and provided medical compensation for cases of serious illnesses. The teams performed dental and eye check-ups and provided medication. This campaign led to the treatment of thousands of students in different cities and villages of Gujarat.

The epicentre of the Bhuj earthquake, a place named 'Kutch' translates to 'a place that alternately becomes wet and dry'. The Rann of Kutch, which covers a major part of this district, was a shallow wetland during the rains and extremely dry during other seasons. It was a difficult place without electricity and water facilities, and had few industries or sources of farming. Officers got scared if they were offered postings in Kutch in those days.

In the days that followed, this very district was transformed by Anandiben and Modi. It all began with Anandiben's initiative of establishing Kutch University. She knew that many students travelled from Kutch to Ahmedabad in order to pursue education, which was a big challenge. On her suggestion, a bill was passed to start the Krantiguru Shyamji Krishna Verma Kachchh University. This, in turn, attracted many private institutions and industries that offered to help in any way to provide employment and facilitate the development of the district.

The state of Gujarat was formed in 1960, but shockingly, it took 40 years to establish a department for the welfare of women and children. The preceding Congress government had not paid any attention to that demographic in the last four decades. Anandiben elected Sushriben Patel as the first director of the WCD department and advocated many issues like domestic violence, dowry and education. Her work made her popular in both rural and urban areas of Gujarat.

Anandiben started the Nari Adalat, a courtroom dedicated to

the issues related to women. Women living in rural areas had little knowledge of laws and lesser resources to hire lawyers to fight their cases. This initiative gave them a free and accessible platform to resolve conflicts in a lawful manner. Anandiben recruited women from within the villages who were involved in social work to resolve the cases internally. She gave them spaces in government offices that were accessible to women. From awareness programmes about family planning to legal issues, the adalat supported women in all. Today, more than 50 such courtrooms are operating in Gujarat, solving issues of many women in the state.

Anandiben's life had solely come to include her work for the people. She hardly remembers any momentous memory from her personal life following her taking charge of the education ministry. Her exemplary achievements in the field of education, and women and child development were not easy. She worked for 16–18 hours a day, with the rest of the day devoted to physical exercise, eating and sleep. For her, work was the purpose of life. Her son was settled with his family, and her daughter was engaged in social work. Her husband had started living in a separate house since Anandiben was mostly travelling or working at the office. Although her children were never a cause of heartache for her, in being away from home, working and serving the people, she missed a lot of the normal family routine.

The love, care and understanding she shares with her children to date are praiseworthy. Anandiben recalls that her children would mostly talk about their school and friends when they sat down to discuss events as a family. They were very sincere. They would greet guests in her absence and make food for them. They would take care of everything around the house. They have always been responsible, perhaps because they saw their mother working hard to make ends meet, and have never complained. They would also help with household chores. Anandiben would get complaints about her children having got into fights with other children, but some of the complaints were so funny that they would bring a smile to her face.

Just like her own children, Anandiben also shares a very good relationship with her grandson, Dharma, and granddaughter, Sanskruti. Dharma, Shwetank's son, was born when she was a Rajya Sabha MP. Anandiben would play with him whenever she got the opportunity. She always told her grandchildren they were free to choose what they wanted to study and who they wanted as life partners.

Anandiben would teach Sanskruti when she was a child. She would talk to her, shop with her, and shares a great bond with her even today. She would also help her select her wardrobe for big ceremonies and meetings.

Anandiben had met Dharma's girlfriend when he was seeing her, who he then married eventually. She is Devendra Patel's daughter, who is a journalist and author (of Gujarati literature) with *Sandesh*, the premier and largest-circulated daily in the Gujarati language. He wrote against the BJP, Modi and even Anandiben. But she did not say no to the marriage. It was only later that Devendra Patel realized how Anandiben and her family are.

There were endless discussions about revamping the education system and Anandiben's suggestions were focused on inculcating India's values and culture in the education of children. She wanted the system to be value-based rather than just informative. She wanted the schools to teach kindness and compassion to all children. She created avenues within the education framework for children to cultivate trust and honesty. The government proposed schools to open a shop that would be run by students for students, where they could purchase and manage inventory of stationery material.

Many schools welcomed the initiative, and the proposal was set in motion. On inspection, it was found that the inventory was indeed very well managed by students in many schools. They named the inventory-keeping project 'Ram's Stationery'. Anandiben believed that if one entrusts responsibilities to children, they will never fail. This method in particular imparted value-based education where students faithfully fulfilled their responsibilities.

Once, Anandiben was visiting a higher-secondary public school in Mehsana, a district in north Gujarat. The school was celebrating its annual day and students and parents were present in large numbers. A young boy of Class IV was being felicitated for securing first position in a game of chess. Anandiben was informed that the boy was excellent at the game but was unable to participate further at the national level due to poor financial conditions. On hearing this, she promptly swung into action and asked her officers to look into the matter. She also called an industrialist and suggested that he sponsor the child. The student eventually participated at the international level and won medals for the nation. The boy became the pride of Gujarat and was later adopted by the same industrialist who had sponsored him. Anandiben prioritized supporting talented children who were deprived of resources to move forward in life.

During her tenure at the WCD department, she made regular visits to Nari Kendras at different places like Surat, Godhra and others. She inspected the facilities and the condition of women. She sat and talked to them for hours, understanding their situation. She arranged for skill training for many women and provided livelihood to those living in these Nari Kendras. There, certain lapses in implementation came to light, but Anandiben kept a firm hold on everything. She promptly summoned those officials who had failed to manage the shelter homes properly. Her strict and firm behaviour was criticized at times, but everyone knew deep down that she was right in her approach.

The year 2002 saw a significant development in law-and-order reforms. The Prevention of Terrorism Act was brought into effect by the Vajpayee administration to provide greater powers to the government authorities investigating and acting against suspects of terrorism. There were concerns about the misuse of this law but it was passed in a joint session of Parliament.

This was followed by major economic reforms in late 2002 and 2003. The BJP government pushed the country's GDP growth to exceed 7 per cent annually from 2003 to 2007. This was after the last three years had registered growth of less than 5 per cent.[4] The government successfully fuelled an increase in foreign investment, revamped public and industrial infrastructure and created job opportunities. The country's economy was favoured by good crop harvests, a rising IT industry and industrial expansion. India was

---

[4]'GDP Growth Annual (%) - India', World Bank, https://bit.ly/3QvRLcF/. Accessed on 9 August 2022.

projecting an urban and modernized international image.

These factors indicated that the NDA would manage to retain power in the 2004 general election, but, unfortunately, many top-tier party leaders and Cabinet Ministers were defeated and the BJP managed only 138 seats out of 543—the coalition scoring only 185 seats in total. The Congress with 145 seats became the single-largest party and with its allies formed the United Progressive Alliance accounting for 220 seats in Parliament. Vajpayee resigned as the prime minister for Dr Manmohan Singh to take up the post.

Transforming Gujarat

Live as if you were to die tomorrow.
Learn as if you were to live forever.

—Mahatma Gandhi

In the four years that Anandiben was in power, she transformed the lives of the people of Gujarat. Across villages and cities, everyone was witness to her allegiance to service and dedication towards work on the ground. She had shown the nation what she was made of.

She once visited a village in a tribal area called Dang. The lack of basic infrastructure in the place shocked her. There were no facilities for children, no water, no toilets; in fact, there were no proper schools. There was a small designated area where around 30 children would come to study. Many children suffered from malnutrition due to scarcity of food. Anandiben realized that there were many districts like Dang where the situation was unfortunately similar. Anandiben expressly directed the local MLAs to use their area development funds to build schools in these tribal areas. She then held a meeting with renowned private school trustees and told them, 'If you can bring quality education to tribal areas, only then will I call you educationists.'

Just like people adopt children, Anandiben's solution saw schools adopting children for the first time. Following her proposal, many areas were adopted by private institutions. The Congress opposed the privatization of schools in villages but Anandiben was clear about her goal. According to her, something was better than nothing. She issued a rule book for private schools that were given the responsibility of government schools in the villages. The schools were not allowed to charge any fee either for academics or for food. The schools in Dang district were adopted by industrialists from Surat. Gradually, many children living in these tribal areas got admission and shelter in the schools. They were given books, uniforms and other facilities by the schools. Organizations like Swaminarayan Sampradaya and philanthropists like Ramesh Bhai Ojha adopted schools. More than 300 schools in the backward areas and hinterlands of Gujarat were adopted and transformed because of this initiative. This was another proof of Anandiben's visionary leadership.

Anandiben worked to ensure children's nutrition and development along with education. In the same way, she wanted to empower women to help them live with dignity in an environment free of discrimination and violence. She categorically improved the nutritional and overall health status of children below six years. She also laid the foundation for proper psychological, physical and social development of a child, and successfully worked towards reducing the incidence of mortality, morbidity and malnutrition.

During her inspection visits, she also comprehended the urgent need for improving the quality of midday meals provided in schools. She received many complaints about the food almost regularly, which had sadly been ignored for many years. Anandiben took a lesson from a method the Bengaluru-based organization Akshaya Patra had implemented to solve a similar problem. The organization served healthy and hygienic meals in the schools of the city. Anandiben visited their kitchen in Bengaluru and was amazed to see how beautifully the staff operated the kitchen. She met the people who managed Akshaya Patra and collaborated with them to serve good-quality food in Gujarat schools as well.

Soon, modern kitchens were established in Gujarat to prepare and distribute meals in schools. The first kitchen was inaugurated by Chief Minister Modi and he keenly oversaw the processes. He offered many suggestions to improve on the initiative, and fed the children with his hands. He asked Anandiben to establish such kitchens in the entire state. Eventually, the food reached all the anganwadis as well. Lakhs of students benefited from nutritional meals with this initiative across the state. Akshaya Patra's work garnered a lot of praise in the entire country. Steadily, issues like malnutrition looked near resolution with such encouraging steps.

In 2003, the state was poised to witness the launch of Modi's grand vision—Vibrant Gujarat: Global Investors' Summit 2003. The summit was organized in Ahmedabad and Surat, the twin commercial cities, during the annual Navratri festival. The state government collaborated with the Centre along with the United Nations Industrial Development Organization (UNIDO), the Federation of Indian Chambers of Commerce and Industry (FICCI) and the Confederation of Indian Industries (CII).

The convention included seminars, exhibitions and discussions on all the industrial sectors of the state. From agriculture and biotech to gems, mining and even infrastructure, several project proposals were tabled and examined between investors and the government. The summit also had international credit rating agencies, leading private- and public-sector banks proving financial advice and support.

The 2003 summit saw 76 memorandums of understanding or MoUs signed with ₹66,068 crore billion promised in investment. The participation of almost 45 countries, hundreds of foreign delegates and major government and industry leaders made the summit a resounding success—one that would be repeated every two years from then on.

During the summit, Anandiben's responsibility was furthering school education policies and framework. She conducted seminars for teachers and students explaining how Gujarat was going to witness drastic change. The arrival of investors in various sectors meant expansion that would create job opportunities for many. This was a golden period for the state. She also signed MoUs for establishing much-needed new technological and medical universities, and smart schools in the state.

In keeping with these large aims, Anandiben started the Apni Tehsil, Vibrant Tehsil (ATVT) campaign at the district level under the guidance of Chief Minister Modi. The successful implementation of government schemes at the ground level made it very important that human resources were strengthened from the ground up at every level. Even holistically designed processes and carefully planned strategies can fail if the implementers are not working at every level. Hence, the tehsil-level programme was launched to provide a 360-degree view of the work. Everyone was involved in the process, from local police officers to collectors, and it made them more responsible and enthusiastic about their work—Anadiben knew the importance of making workers on the ground feel appreciated.

Improvising things at the district level impacted the speed of work at the state level. The ATVT manuals were published and distributed in all the districts. Many issues got resolved at the lower stages due to the ATVT initiative, which worked on five key parameters: social and infrastructure survey, identification of the missing links, conversions of schemes and teamwork.

The 12th legislative elections held in the year 2007 brought the BJP back to power with 117 seats out of a total of 182. Modi was successfully leading the party and ably governing the state as the results proved.

Anandiben, too, was evolving as one of the most trusted leaders in the state. Her rise was visible with the work she was doing. She won the Patan seat for the third time in a row, which is a huge achievement.

In addition to Education and WCD, Anandiben was assigned Roads and Building, and Revenue in her third term. It was a both a surprise and responsibility for her. It was a clear outcome of the exemplary work that she had undertaken as an education minister in her previous terms. Modi backed Anandiben and trusted her capabilities to the fullest, given her proven track record. He knew that despite her limited knowledge of the new ministries, she would still be able to completely transform the status with due diligence. Anandiben moved forward with Modi's guidance and the blessings of her family, and assumed office.

Understanding the new ministries was a huge challenge for her, but like always, she took it in her stride. As is characteristic of her dedication towards work, Anandiben's stint in the ministry of roads and building led to many high-impact projects. Patan was connected with the Narmada canal for the welfare of farmers in addition to creating 174 check dams in the region and a massive drinking water filtration plant. A new medical and engineering college was also constructed in the region. Under her term, a more than 700-kilometre-long network of roads and underground drainage systems were built.

Nitin Patel was the irrigation minister at the time. The teams that were selected to do the work would give presentations to the Cabinet Ministers about the Narmada issue. Just when Anandiben thought she had nothing to do with the issue at hand, one evening, she got an order from Modiji that she had to oversee the work.

Anandiben had a lot of departments under her, but Modiji gave her this important task because he knew that only she could pull it off. It took her 1.5 years to complete the work.

Anandiben supported the farmers throughout the process, both personally and legally. She would stay the night with them and have dinner. The villagers were so happy that they would cook special food for her.

The PWD constructed the road and bridge after the survey. After all this work, the farmers began to trust the government and Anandiben's efforts. She would not just talk about their land but also address their other needs. Her method would be to write down what kind of things the work under her departments required and get them done accordingly.

As the canal was getting built, farmers could see the changes happening around them. Anandiben wanted to visit a village where a majority of the people were Muslims. While some conveyed their apprehensions about this trip, she went ahead undeterred. She sat with everyone and encouraged them to share their problems. After a few hours, they cooked food for her when she told them she was hungry. Women made bajra rotis for Anandiben and other officials at midnight. They said it was the first time a minister had visited them. She heard their issues and ordered the officers to solve them immediately, like translating English forms into Gujarati.

During her work term in the revenue ministry, Anandiben noticed several discrepancies internally. There were instances of delayed work, rampant corruption and exchange of unnecessary favours in the departments. People had to wait in long queues to get even the smallest of jobs done. Anandiben observed that the people of the state struggled to enjoy the benefits of the schemes provided by the government. What was the point of coming up with schemes if the benefit from them was so hard to come by? Her upbringing, childhood idols and ideals in her life were the source of her principles and she knew from the very start that she would not tolerate such dishonest practices.

This was why the Jan Seva Kendras came to be. The aim of such centres was to provide instant solutions related to land and revenue problems faced by the citizens. The centres were opened at accessible locations in different cities and villages. She gave special focus to using the latest IT systems to speed up work that, in turn, reduced human effort and saved a lot of time. The government collaborated with the National Informatics Centre (NIC) and developed digital infrastructure for the revenue department and trained its officers. The government to citizens or G2C service became an example of e-governance in Gujarat. All it took was some initiative and drive by a visionary leader who believes in putting the people and her nation first.

In many villages of the country, the Khasra Girdawari system, which is a legal document accepted by the revenue department, was in use. It specifies land, crop and ownership details and is considered to be very important. To maintain these records, the e-Dhara Kendra was launched by Anandiben. Within a period of six months, the records of more than 14 lakh villages were computerized. As e-Dhara digitally documented all the physical records, automatic maintenance and updates were scheduled to ease out the process.

Anandiben had lived the life of a common man, growing up as the daughter of a farmer and earning her livelihood as a teacher. She had lived all the struggles that a citizen faced. Her vision was to save people's time by making processes efficient and straightforward.

Two hundred and twenty-five districts across the state got centres dedicated to e-Dhara services. It was a challenge to make the physical process digital but it steadily transformed the way things functioned. It bypassed land mafias, corrupt middlemen and others who exploited citizens to get their work done. The e-Dhara system became an integral part of e-governance. It prompted the launch of similar projects like e-registration and AnyRoR (Any Records of Rights Anywhere in Gujarat) to check land records and help farmers maintain online records of their land and revenue.

The most memorable experience during her stint in these new ministries was the construction of the Narmada canal. After much criticism and dissension, when Chief Minister Modi was reviewing the canal work, it was obvious that a lot of hard work had gone into the construction.

Anandiben remembers that the water tunnel constructed near Kevadia supplied water from Ahmedabad to Saurashtra, Kutch and even to some places in Rajasthan. However, the issue was that the network needed to connect these water channels to the farms was not ready by then. The building of this network through small canals required land, that too from the farmers. It was decided that the government would pay 30 per cent more than the rate of the land and 80 per cent of that amount would be paid in cash.[5] The historic decision was taken after consultation with the farmers and they happily offered their land.

Anandiben personally visited more than 12 districts in this connection and went to all the villages to meet with the farmers. She listened to the issues of the farmers and communicated those to the Chief Minister. She stayed with them throughout the process

[5] 'Gujarat to Pay New "Jantri" Rate, Plus 30% Compensation, to Farmers for Land Coming under Narmada Canal Network', *Gujarat Samachar*, https://bit.ly/3pbDiqx. Archived on 12 June 2011. Accessed on 9 August 2022.

at all times and under all conditions. She understood their concerns and acted wisely in favour of the farmers. After fetching 60 per cent of the land requirement, the tender was issued and the canal began construction. She worked in close collaboration with the irrigation department and the PWD.

When farmers saw the benefits of the canal, they started offering portions of their land for the remaining channel network. After her consistent hard work for years, one lakh farmers gave one lakh hectare land for the Narmada canal project. Everyone was surprised at the immensity of the project and how she had managed to pull it off. Only a few people knew that Anandiben, being the daughter of a farmer herself, was able to identify with the pains of a farmer. She knew what the farmers needed. She stood with them and assured support, and lived up to her promises. She resolved more than 800 court cases related to canal land acquisitions. To this day, she feels blessed to be a part of this journey of building the Narmada canal. It is a career highlight for her.

Anandiben had a very systemic approach to work. She always started work at the foundation level because she knew that building on a strong base resulted in the best and most reliable future projects. While working for the roads and building ministry, Anandiben focused on the development of the villages, especially those that were affected due to heavy rains. She surveyed the entire state and observed how rains affected the education, health and infrastructure of the villages for months.

She then started a project called 'Maroon Village'. It was decided that all the villages that were marooned or isolated during the monsoons would be connected to highways to strengthen the exit plan to save the villagers, in case of a calamity. The budget allotted to the project amounted to ₹250 crore. It was used to build roads and bridges in many villages. Slowly, the number of marooned villages in the state reduced and, finally, came down to zero. The project benefited her village, Kharod, as well. She shares that the experience of building roads in Kharod was a special one. The village had had no roads since Independence. The people expressed gratitude to Anandiben for her efforts to improve the conditions of villages.

Another exemplary initiative by Anandiben was the Sakhi Mandal platform which garnered praise across the state. Her commitment to uplifting women was encouraged by Modi's views that a country whose women are empowered can never falter in its growth. Taking this vision forward, self-help groups named Sakhi Mandal were created that helped women receive financial loans and livelihood support through established platforms for exposure. Women started investing in the programme and reaped many benefits. More than 50,000 Sakhi Mandals were formed in Gujarat.

The platform enabled women to sell products and other creations in exhibitions. Villages started holding festivals showcasing their culture and innovation. Eventually, they started small businesses supported by the government. Many women learnt and earned through Sakhi Mandals. A few received primary education, and even became the sarpanch of the village. Anandiben also established the Mahila Suraksha Samiti, where women supported other women in times of crisis. The samiti also held self-defence training and awareness programmes to help against domestic violence.

Anandiben's political career was steered by her own principles as well as through the many gems of humanity she came across, who taught her to always remain committed to social service. Such people were always active to serve, without caring for personal joy, happiness or comfort. Anandiben had entered politics in 1987 and, at the time, few women participated in active politics. When she had taken up the charge of the Gujarat Mahila Morcha, there was an incident involving one woman named Annapurnaben from Kalol town of Mehsana district.

Annapurnaben was a poor but very hard-working widow with two sons. She worked tirelessly for the party during elections, often losing out on sleep. She earned her livelihood by selling milk pouches. With time, Anandiben had lost contact with Annapurnaben, but her service and loyalty remained etched in her mind.

After many years, Anandiben met Annapurnaben when she was called to Kalol for a function organized by the BJP. She was extremely happy to see her, but Annapurnaben's condition was pathetic. Anandiben took out the time to go to her home, where she learnt that one of Annapurnaben's sons had passed away and the other was facing challenges with employment. Anandiben offered immediate financial and other material assistance and left. She was deeply disturbed to know the condition of such a hard-working party member.

After a few months, Annapurnaben came to Anandiben's house and shared how piteous her condition was: she did not have the resources to buy food for the next day.

'What happened?' Anandiben asked.

'Ben, you know that I would never ask for help. This is the first time I am asking for something. I beg you to save my younger son.

He took a loan from the bank but our income is not sufficient to pay back the loan,' Annapurnaben implored with folded hands.

As she narrated her struggle, Anandiben reflected on Ananpurnaben's contributions to the party. She remembered that Modi had told her to always stand with the party workers in their time of need and that is what she did.

'Tell me how I can help.'

'Just give me rations for some time. I will pay it back once our instalments are paid.'

Anandiben fought back tears and said with a lump in her throat, 'Don't worry, I am with you.'

Anandiben could understand how difficult the times must be for a self-respecting person like Annapurnaben to beg for aid. She was a dedicated worker of the party and as a senior leader, Anandiben took care of her well-being. She asked Shri Ashok Desai, her personal assistant, to procure and deliver all the material to Annapurnaben to her home in Kalol. Anandiben then hugged her and said, 'You are an inspiration for people like me. I learnt dedication and commitment from you. You don't worry; I am always here for you.' They both shed tears as Annapurnaben bade goodbye. After two years, she came back to thank Anandiben and told her that her loans had been paid and she was in a better condition.

Such incidents show that Anandiben was beyond a politician or a leader. She worked with the heart of a mother—caring and strict in equal measure. Her kindness and compassion were something rarely seen in politics. She proudly gives credit for her principles and visions to her father and Modi.

Anandiben's relationship with Ashok Desai, who is the officer on special duty (OSD) now, is also worth mentioning here. This working relationship is based on trust, something that has been developed over the years. Ashok was introduced to the family as a friend, specifically to Anandiben, by Jayesh Patel, her son-in-law. Ashok, a mechanical engineer by profession, had always been interested in politics, and both he and Jayesh were supporters of the BJP. He had joined Anandiben's team during the first Legislative Assembly election and had campaigned for her with Jayesh and Anar. They would go to villages and do surveys. After winning, Jayesh suggested that Desai join Anandiben's team full-time. He got associated in 1998 and has been working with her since. He is one of her most trusted associates.

The 15th Lok Sabha elections of 2009 placed the Congress-led UPA with a strong majority. The defeat of the BJP at the Centre did not faze the state-level work of the party.

Anandiben worked relentlessly in the ministries of education, WCD, roads and building, and revenue. In her tenure spanning almost a decade, the citizens could see a complete transformation and revival of the state: there were no long queues to claim benefits; there was no wait time involved in getting local issues resolved; corruption had seen a major downturn; and no scams had been reported. A happy and healthy state was all Anandiben had dreamt of, actively worked for and achieved.

The Gujarat government and the state election commission introduced e-voting for the 2010 local body elections. Gujarat became the first state to hold online elections. On the other hand, the election campaign intensified with the Central Bureau of Investigation (CBI) arresting Amit Shah in the Sohrabuddin Sheikh fake encounter case. The BJP alleged that the arrest amounted to misuse of the CBI by the Congress and urged the people to give a fitting reply by casting their votes.[6]

The Congress focused on the corporation polls being about civic amenities and highlighted assistance given to the state under the Jawaharlal Nehru Urban Renewal Mission. However, the current political developments and the BJP's spectacular track record of development in the state won them the battle.

All the six municipal corporations—Ahmedabad, Surat, Rajkot, Vadodara, Jamnagar and Bhavnagar—were retained by the BJP with ease. Contesting his communal image, Chief Minister Modi said after the results, 'Even Muslims voted for the Gujarat BJP. We have managed to win their hearts and that reflects in our huge victory.'[7]

Although these were civic polls, the scale of the campaign was unprecedented in comparison. Anandiben herself addressed about six rallies a day in the run-up to the elections. The focus was firmly on the development brought about by the Modi government, and even national leaders like Sushma Swaraj and Nitin Gadkari came to remind voters of it.

As it is with development, so is it with politics—strategies need to be implemented with careful planning. The focus was on

---

[6]'BJP Leaders Court Arrest Protesting Misuse of CBI', *The Indian Express*, 12 May 2010, https://bit.ly/3JFz5Vw. Accessed on 9 August 2022.

[7]'Muslims Also Voted for Us in Kathlal: Narendra Modi', *DNA*, 13 October 2010, https://bit.ly/3p6OaGe. Accessed on 9 August 2022.

the next challenge, that of the 2012 Gujarat Legislative Assembly elections. Modi, the chief minister since 2002, was running for his fourth term.

The BJP was positive about another win in the state as the government had implemented the best policies and schemes for the benefit of its people. Surely, the citizens of Gujarat were impressed with the developments, especially in education, roads and revenue departments. In the 2012 elections, Anandiben was given the ticket from a newly formed constituency, Ghatlodiya. It is located in Ahmedabad and came into existence after the 2008 delimitation.

Anandiben's campaign was all about her work in the ministries, which she had been in charge of for five years. There was not much for her to talk about since all her hard work was in front of the voters to see. The elections witnessed a record voter turnout, the highest since 1980.[8] The results were in favour of the BJP, led by Modi, with 116 seats.

The Congress was limited to 60 seats, and former Gujarat chief minister and ex-BJP member Keshubhai Patel's Gujarat Parivartan Party (GPP) managed only two seats. Keshubhai's sole intention of opposing Modi did not bear fruit but a victorious and humble Modi did not fail to seek his blessings at Gandhinagar.

The BJP's resounding victory was not just a validation of the statewide popularity of Modi and his efforts towards development, it was an indication towards the making of a visionary leader who

[8]'Gujarat Assembly Elections 2017: 68% Turnout in Phase 1, Voting in 89 Constituencies Ends', *India.com*, 9 December 2017, https://bit.ly/3zAtfAk. Accessed on 9 August 2022.

was increasingly seeming to be the ideal prime ministerial candidate for the 2014 general elections.

It was no surprise then that Anandiben won the maiden Ghatlodiya constituency seat against Prahladbhai Patel from the Congress. The fact that she won with a margin of 175,000 votes was unprecedented. She was congratulated by Modi and other senior leaders for this victory, who were now even more confident about her capabilities. In the new term, Anandiben continued as the Cabinet Minister of roads and building, and revenue. In addition, Modi assigned her urban development and urban housing, disaster management, and capital projects.

Villages in Gujarat were rapidly being urbanized after Independence, and the expansion of cities was also being accelerated extensively under Anandiben's leadership. The urban development and urban housing departments geared up as soon as she assumed office. She formulated new policies in discussion with S.S. Rathore, the additional chief secretary, and other officials in matters related to revenue, urban development and housing, and also monitored their implementation. Given her work towards reform, her supporters often claimed that after Todar Mal, who was the finance minister during Akbar's reign, it was Anandiben who had the potential to transform the revenue department of Gujarat.

Anandiben had always shown promise. The spark that Modi had seen in her was missing in a lot of others. It wasn't just her hard work that impressed Modi, but the hard work that bore the right results and was always aimed at the welfare of the people. He could visualize Anandiben walking in his footsteps and continuing to take care of the state and its people with honesty and integrity.

He saw his reflection in Anandiben—his values and commitment to the nation. Her unstinting journey from party worker to Cabinet Minister, no doubt, made her an ideal potential candidate for the chief minister chair.

When Modi was due to leave for Delhi to work on the 2014 Lok Sabha elections, he called Anandiben along with Saurabh Patel, Nitin Patel and Bhupendrasinh Chudasama. Modi appointed Anandiben as the chairperson of the four-member ministerial group formed to run the show in Gujarat in his absence.

Despite winning elections for the fourth time in a row, Anandiben's nature and vision were aligned with the welfare of the society. She credited her rise in politics to the people who trusted her work rather than giving in to self-importance. As a ritual of gratitude, she often visited Visnagar to seek Saritaben's blessings. Over the years, she had lost most of her siblings, but her relationship with Manguben had remained strong even after she joined active politics, and she often spent time with her in Ahmedabad. She hardly had time for a personal life, but she never sidelined her family. She visited her village and met with her brothers and sisters whenever an opportunity presented itself. Everyone respected her work and her time. No one in her family, including her children, ever had to complain about her busy schedule or their neglect thereof. Amidst all these, it was only Anandiben's husband, Mafatlal, who slowly lost his position, both in politics and in her life.

In her new constituency, her dedication to her work became evident through an interesting incident. Anandiben was on her way to attend an inauguration event of a primary school when she noticed that the officials were taking her through, what looked like, a long route. When she inquired why the route had been changed, the officers hesitantly told her that the usual road was not alright. This raised her suspicions and she insisted on diverting the convoy and going by the original route, mostly used by the children and teachers to travel. It was then that she saw that the condition of the road was pathetic: it was kuchha (not laid with concrete) and full of potholes. She immediately called the officers of the Ahmedabad Nagar Nigam who were responsible for its maintenance and asked them the reason for the lack of repair. She demanded a report within a week. The road was repaired within the month.

Anandiben delayed neither her decisions nor her work. She believes that we must do things now or never at all. She has similarly resolved many such cases where immediate actions and approvals were required. Her quick thinking and logical decision-making has often been praised by citizens.

When Anandiben took charge of the urban development and urban housing department, it led to the implementation of many schemes and projects. All this was done to raise the standard of living. In Gujarat, about 50 per cent of the population lived in small private colonies. In slums and other low-class areas, the MLA fund was used to build roads, street lights and other work, but the problem was with the private colonies where the fund couldn't be used due to some restrictions. The people living in the private colonies were people from the lower middle class. First, Anandiben took steps towards the welfare of this section of the population. She directed a comprehensive survey of such colonies to figure out the common problems. She met with the people and discussed their views while her team created an action plan to resolve the issues. Within two years, the budget and plan were executed and the private colonies were revamped for good. People praised Anandiben's planning and implementation efforts for the betterment of this class of society.

Another big milestone in Anandiben's tenure as the urban development and urban housing minister was the town planning scheme. In 2012, during her meeting with the officials of the ministry, the most pressing issue that came to the fore was that of pending approvals for more than 450 projects. The projects related to town planning were of utmost importance for the overall development of the state. Many people had suffered due to the delay of such projects and, in turn, the officials had also had to face their wrath. There was also suspicion of rampant corruption.

Given the situation, Anandiben got to work immediately and devised a plan to resolve the issue. She asked to meet all the housing officers and town planners to discuss the issues in person. They were asked to bring with them all relevant documents. Anandiben sat with the engineers and understood the project plan and architecture. After working day and night, more than 100 plans were approved and finalized. In cities like Ahmedabad, Baroda and Surat, many projects were executed and completed within a very short span of time. More than 250 plans were implemented during Anandiben's tenure. Such was her zeal for work and service.

She continued her work to provide essential health services to young children, pregnant women and lactating mothers, and adolescent girls through anganwadis. She also focused on preventing female foeticide and to ensure the survival, education and protection of the girl child. Her department worked on providing shelter, police desks, and legal, medical and counselling services to female or child victims of abuse and/or violence.

India displayed dismal figures when it came to undernutrition. It was worse for the girl child, and the problems were compounded by early marriage and pregnancies in villages. Miscarriages and other serious health issues were common and families could not afford healthy food and provide hygienic conditions to pregnant women. While the government launched many schemes to reduce the occurrence of such cases through anganwadis, health camps and other necessary provisions, the situation did not improve even after several efforts.

When Anandiben was at the helm, a meeting of doctors from different fields was called. Many key decisions were taken, starting from an improved method of measuring malnutrition to supporting children and educating them in order to improve their eating habits. Children were categorized into different coloured zones according to their health status and the action required. Diet charts were created for children and medicines were given to undernourished women. In collaboration with Amul, a nutritional paste was launched in Gujarat, named 'Bal Amritayam'. Anandiben explored all avenues and put all approaches to work; she did not rest until a solution was found.

The First Woman Chief Minister

Satisfaction lies in the effort, not in the attainment,
full effort is full victory.

—Mahatma Gandhi

The BJP geared up for the Lok Sabha elections in 2014 and announced Modi as their official candidate for prime minister. Meanwhile, in Gujarat, Anandiben emerged as Modi's successor after successfully running the government in his absence as the head of the group of ministers tasked with running the state's day-to-day affairs while Modi was away campaigning.

Modi's candidature as the next prime minister drew opposition from several BJP leaders even though he played a dominant role in the election campaign. An individual focus was an unusual phenomenon for a BJP election campaign and this was being heralded as the 'Modi wave' in India. The 2014 election looked like a referendum on Narendra Modi.

During the campaign, Modi focused on corruption scandals under the incumbent Congress government, and worked on his image as a politician who brought about the Gujarat model of development. His message of neoliberal ideology along with Hindutva found support among young Indians and middle-class citizens. The BJP successfully shifted the national consensus from doubts about secularism towards development and progress. With regard to campaign methods, Modi made extensive use of social media and technology like hologram appearances in rallies along with conventional methods.

The *Ab ki baar, Modi sarkar* wave proved to be the general elections with the highest voter turnout in the political history of India.[9] The BJP more than doubled its seat tally in the Lok Sabha to 282, while their alliance won 336 seats in the 543-seat Lok Sabha. The results shattered the Congress's dominance in Indian politics and ushered in a new political order. In Gujarat, the BJP won all 26 seats. The entire nation celebrated this victory, hopeful for a new India.

Narendra Modi had earned the leadership of not only the party but also of the nation. On 26 May 2014, he was appointed the prime minister of India. In his first speech, he pledged to work for his countrymen, saying, 'Brothers, sisters, you have faith in me and I have faith in you... The people of this country have given their verdict. This verdict says we have to make the dreams of 1.25 billion people come true. I must work hard.'[10]

---

[9]Jain, Bharti, 'Highest Ever Voter Turnout Recorded in 2014 Polls', *The Times of India*, 13 May 2013, https://bit.ly/3djUkQU. Accessed on 9 August 2022.

[10]Elliot, John, 'India's NaMo Picks His Team', *Newsweek*, 20 May 2014, https://bit.ly/3OZsmIp. Accessed on 6 May 2022.

Modi had been the chief minister of Gujarat for more than a decade, therefore, before submitting his resignation to Governor Kamla Beniwal, Modi had attended a special session of the State Legislative Assembly where he was accorded a farewell by the members. In his farewell speech, he had said, 'I am sure Gujarat is now on the path to success. The praise one gets from his own people is most valuable. I faced a lot of challenges when I was appointed the chief minister. I was fortunate to have been elected the chief minister of Gujarat. The results we have witnessed are because of the Gujarat model. I am indebted to everyone for their kind words.'[11]

During the special assembly session after Modi's success as the prime ministerial candidate, Anandiben said, 'It is a day of pride for Gujarat that its son will be the PM of India. Narendra Modi will take the country to new heights.' She was extremely proud and happy to see her mentor and friend become the next prime minister. She had closely observed his journey, struggles and passion for serving the nation. He was one of the major reasons Anandiben had been able to gather courage and work in politics for such a long time. For her, the mandate was a blessing for India.

According to the media, as Modi stepped down from Gujarat, Anandiben was the most likely choice for the next chief minister of the state. She had been second in command during Modi's national campaigning absence and had a decade-long stint in state politics. Although, Finance Minister Nitin Patel and Modi's confidant, Amit

---

[11]'Narendra Modi Bids Farewell to Gujarat', *The Times of India*, 21 May 2014, https://bit.ly/3Pac26y. Accessed on 9 August 2022.

Shah, were also in the race, Anandiben seemed to be the popular choice. The media even reached her village and took interviews of the people.

On the other end, Anandiben had neither the inclination nor interest in becoming the chief minister. She had never considered power to be a part of the equation she had with her work—she was content to work wherever she was placed and felt grateful to fulfil her duties in an upstanding manner. Rather than inquiring about her prospects or discussing her candidature, she focused on the tasks that needed to be completed.

On a regular work day, Anandiben sat in the Kamalam BJP office going through some files when a senior leader of the party working alongside her asked, 'Madam, when are you taking the oath?'

'Oath? For what?'

'You don't know? Your name has been proposed as the next chief minister.'

Anandiben was taken aback at the information. 'Who told you?'

'The news is everywhere. Everyone knows it.'

She did not know how to react to the news. In all fairness, she had gotten some hints through media coverage and other party workers, but had not expected it to really happen. She was perplexed rather than excited and needed time to digest the information.

Later, she got a confirmation call from Bhupendrasinh Chudasama, the then law minister of Gujarat. True to her personality, she did not celebrate, but started planning her next steps.

Anandiben called her children over for dinner and broke the news to them matter-of-factly. There was no display of achievement, not even a special dish or delicacy to mark the occasion, and as a testimony to Anandiben's diligent parenting, even Shewtank and Anar did not make a fuss about their mother climbing to the highest rank in state politics.

Like all the other times Anandiben had achieved success, her husband continued to be a thorn in her side. Saritaben was upset about the media articles and Mafatbhai's constant nagging. He had been complaining to her siblings about Anandiben's behaviour, even though all her siblings knew what the truth was. Saritaben's advice to Anandiben was to file for divorce and end this painful chapter of her life. When Mafatbhai got to know about it, he called Anandiben's brother and said he did not want a divorce.

On the professional front, though, nobody doubted Anandiben's calibre. Her name was proposed unanimously at a closed-door meeting of the Legislative Party in the presence of Modi, where Amit Shah and Thavar Chand Gehlot, then BJP general secretary, were also present. Later, in a function held at Town Hall, Bhupendrasinh Chudasama officially announced her candidacy. She folded her hands and thanked several hundred BJP members, including MLAs, who accepted her candidacy in the presence of Modi. It was announced that she would soon go to the governor's house to stake her claim as the chief minister.

In the meeting, Modi demonstrated his complete support as he praised Anandiben's work in her ministries. He told everyone about her journey thus far, starting from the day she had joined as the president of the Mahila Morcha. According to him, Anandiben was the most deserving candidate to lead the state. In a reference to Anandiben's stint as a principal, Modi asked the ministers to function with utmost responsibility. She was the longest-serving

BJP minister in the state as she had handled portfolios under both Modi and Keshubhai Patel, and her colleagues knew her to be a strict disciplinarian and a hard task-master.

Saritaben had always been a mother figure in Anandiben's life and Anandiben called her to seek her blessings after the official announcement had been made. 'I will come and see you soon,' Saritaben responded, 'don't worry about me. You have a big responsibility now. Do it with honesty as you always do, just like father taught us.'

Anandiben took oath on 22 May 2014.

Just the day before, Modi had given an emotional speech about the support that he had received from his party. He said, 'You can see Modi not because Modi's stature is very big. You can see Modi because the party's senior leaders have hoisted me on their shoulders.' He continued the speech by listing his priorities, and his promise to work for the poor, youth, women, oppressed and the deprived. The elation of winning the elections with a popular mandate continued.

The chief minister swearing-in ceremony was attended by all senior party leaders along with Modi, who had called all the state Cabinet Ministers and briefed them about the ceremony. Everybody was in attendance—from senior dignitaries to grassroots party workers. The ceremony started as all the guests and to-be Cabinet Ministers took their seats. During the oath-taking ceremony, Anandiben started her speech with, 'I, Anandiben Mafatbhai Patel,' and went on to take the oath. The reason for this was that when Anandiben had filed her nomination papers, she had written her name as Anandiben Mafatbhai Patel. It also showed that when it came to professional commitments, Anandiben remained true to herself and performed her duty diligently, not letting personal issues come into play. As the former chief minister, Prime Minister-elect Modi handed over the charge of the state to Anandiben Patel with much praise of her 16-year-long service to the state and the party. In his speech, he said, 'She will be the first chief minister who has a gold medal in master's in science, and has also received a presidential medal. This is for the first time that Gujarat will get a woman chief minister and I am sure that development under her will be good.'[12]

Anandiben was called to the podium for her acceptance speech. She proudly walked with folded hands, wearing a mud-brown sari. Anandiben adjusted the microphone but before she could say much, she was overcome with emotion. She thanked Modi and other senior leaders for reposing their trust in her and for choosing her to shoulder the responsibility of the entire state. In many ways, Anandiben and Modi shared many common traits between them: their zeal for hard work, dedication to service, deserving rise in politics and deep gratitude towards seniors.

Somewhere in the middle of her speech, Anandiben went blank. She felt a familiar rush as memories from her past flashed in front of her eyes. From her happy childhood days to the struggles that she had faced in her marriage, from her father's words of wisdom to her husband's consistent taunts—all of it came to her at that moment. She remembered all those days when she had thought of giving up but chose not to. She sighed and continued her speech.

---

[12]PTI, 'The Teacher Who Became Gujarat's First Woman Chief Minister', *Financial Express*, 3 August 2016, https://bit.ly/3zFLhBm. Accessed on 9 Auust 2022.

She could not control her tears and expressed her gratitude to the people with a shiver in her voice. She concluded, 'My rise will be an inspiration to women workers in the BJP.'

Governor Kamla Beniwal administered her oath along with a Cabinet of six ministers: Nitin Patel, Ramanlal Vora, Bhupendrasinh Chudasama, Saurabh Patel, Ganpatsinh Vasava and Babubhai Bokhiria. Twenty ministers of state were also sworn in at the same event.

It was one of the biggest oath ceremonies Gujarat had ever witnessed. For the first time in the history of the state, a woman had become the chief minister—one with no influential background but only hard work and perseverance to speak for her; a woman on a mission to serve the people; a woman who had stood against all odds and worked day and night with complete integrity.

Anandiben greeted all the dignitaries at the end. She touched the feet of all the senior leaders and took their blessings. The very next day, she assumed office. Four days later, on 26 May 2014, Modi was sworn in as the 14th prime minister of India.

Since she had not been able to meet Saritaben after her oath-taking ceremony (the date had clashed with Modi's prime ministerial swearing-in), she decided to visit her after an event that was scheduled in Mehsana district. Before she could do so, Anar called Anandiben to inform her that Saritaben was critical and inquire where they should admit her. Anandiben told Anar to take Saritaben to Ahmedabad. In 10 minutes, she got a call from Anar that Saritaben had passed away. They performed Saritaben's last rites in Sidhpur. To this day, Anandiben regrets not having been able to seek Saritaben's blessings.

Anandiben took the news very hard. Losing her was quite a blow to her, and she was inconsolable. Saritaben was her inspiration. She had been like a mother to her. Her words and blessings had been the key sources of energy for Anandiben. Saritaben had always stood by her and guided her when she faced a challenging situation. Her presence had meant a lot, especially after the death of their parents. Anandiben went to Visnagar with her family members and paid her tribute to Saritaben. The memories of the day still make Anandiben emotional.

Anandiben threw herself into her work as soon as she assumed office; she became more assiduous in her work for the state. She turned her attention to reforming governance and wanted to make the administration more streamlined. Carrying Modi's ideology forward, she wanted to make Gujarat a model state for the entire nation. Her mission was to make Gujarat a happy and safe place for its residents and thus focused on fast-tracking the development of the state.

With her strong administrative skills, she influenced the work culture in Gujarat. She declared that any state officials who accepted bribes would be sacked without delay. She was known to be incorruptible; her officers knew that she was a woman of her word who wanted to encourage honesty and integrity.

Anandiben was aware of the issues that an ordinary man could face due to poor governance. She wanted to bring about effective change in order to improve those conditions. For this, she proposed programmes of change that were easily understandable and accessible to all, and yet, technical in their approach. Her initiative of devolving administrative autonomy to local levels away from the state government led to many innovations. For her, development was a mass movement and she wanted Gujarat to be its base.

She had varied experience in managing the education, revenue, roads, PWD, urban development and housing, and WCD ministries. She had proved her capabilities by strengthening all these departments in the last decade. During these years, the most common problem she came across was the delay of work in government offices. She met lakhs of people, and most of the times they would complain about the issues and corruption at the lower level. It was obvious that sometimes it would take months to get a simple job done. Though she had been working towards it in her respective departments, when she became the chief minister, she had the power to get work done in all state government departments. To solve this issue on a wider scale, she thought of initiating a campaign: the Lok Samvad Setu or Lok Darbar.

She made it a point to meet people personally even after becoming the chief minister of the state and strove to provide a fast-tracked solution for their problems. For example, disabled people had to get their disability cards renewed every year. Anandiben knew it was a completely pointless exercise as there were very few people who recovered from their disability in the same year. Even if a few of them did recover, it did not make any sense to have all the disabled people go through the renewal process. Hence, she immediately issued a permanent disability card which saved lakhs of people from having to go through a troublesome process annually.

During the elections, there was a halt in government work for three months. Anandiben came across many pending files and she decided to fast-track the processes to resolve all pending issues. She thought of setting a work target of 100 days for all the departments. The target was the same for everyone, including ministers and high-level bureaucrats: to ensure that maximum work got done within the stipulated deadline.

Anandiben reminded the district administration to ensure that achieving targets should not clash with the benefits expected from the welfare projects and should reach the needy. She started a campaign called Gatisheel Gujarat to fast-track government processes. This campaign is perhaps the shining star among all her achievements during her social and political career.

Anandiben called for a high-level meeting. She greeted the newly appointed Cabinet and announced her idea of setting a 100-day target for major developmental changes. In her own words, 'We are setting a target of 100 days target for a progressive Gujarat to focus on 11 major people-oriented issues, or POI, under 48 administrative heads.' As she finished reading from a paper on her table, it came as a surprise to the officers who were anticipating strict action about pending files and projects. She continued, 'As Modiji has guided us and told us, we have been chosen to serve the people of Gujarat. So, let us start the work immediately.' She closed the file and folded her hands. She had a focused vision of Gujarat's unique development since the day she was sworn in as the chief minister.

The very next day, the media reported on Gujarat's development model being discussed at the national and global level. Announcing the target, government spokespersons, Health Minister Nitinbhai Patel and Finance and Energy Minister Saurabh Patel, said that the objective was to take the state to greater heights. The core aim was to realize the mantra of *'Sauno Saath, Sauno Vikas',* the slogan that was created during the 2014 election campaign, popularly known as *'Sabka Saath, Sabka Vikas* (Everyone's support, everyone's development)'.

The ministers also quoted that Gujarat's administrative set-up had already established its unique identity in the country, as it had then prepared different themes to concentrate on the new targets for the all-round development of the state through proactive administration. It all showed the genius of Anandiben's administrative prowess.

'The targets have been fixed keeping Gujarat's development model in mind, such as Women's Empowerment, Nutritious Gujarat and Mahatma Gandhi Health Mission among other issues. The targets would be widely publicized among six crore people through different channels, public debate, Garib Kalyan Mela, Chintan Shibir and SWAGAT [State-Wide Attention on public Grievance by Application of Technology],' explained Nitin Patel.[13] He added, 'Other issues include modernizing revenue records, prioritizing drinking water, and smooth disposal of solid waste under the Gujarat Urban Mission, the implementation of 100 days' Smart Learning programmes in select 500 schools, strengthening skill development training for the youth and arranging recruitment fairs.'[14]

Anandiben set a special benchmark for the karma yogis (ground-

---

[13]'Gatisheel Gujarat - 100 Days Target', Gandhinagar Portal | Circle of Information, https://bit.ly/3bGb3gF. Accessed on 9 August 2022.

[14]Ibid.

level workers) to attain targets. The training modules had been tuned into electronic learning portals. She organized the entire '100-Day Target' project in such a way, that it had to be implemented under the direct supervision of collectors and district development officers down to the taluka level by separate teams. There was a guardian minister and guardian secretary in each district under whose observation the work was to be done. In addition, a department had been created to assist with appropriate infrastructure for the coordination of different programmes. The sectors shortlisted by the government were soon announced and included areas that were of special interest to Anandiben as well as critical to the economic development of the state.

- The POIs in the sector of women empowerment were looking forward to several activities, notable among them being: the formation of 4,000 new women groups, arranging for their health check-ups and planning for their revolving fund under the Mission Mangalam Project; the formation of 10,000 self-help groups covering housing and employment beneficiaries and their training facilities; setting up conferences for urban women in six districts under the Mission Mangalam Project; distributing cheques to 45,000 beneficiaries under the Kasturba Nutrition Assistance Project; expansion of the Women Security Committee; imparting self-defence training to 26,000 women under the Suraksha Setu Project, etc.
- The Nutritious Gujarat POI focused on the development and nutrition of children and young adults, and its activities included treatment of extremely underweight anganwadi

children under the Child Medical Treatment Centre (CMTC); providing facilities for the medical check-up of all underweight children of anganwadis; planning to arrange nutrition awareness week across villages; imparting training to all the sakhis and sahelis of anganwadis under the *Sabla* scheme; distributing iron and folic acid (IFA) tablets to all needy teenage girls; distributing flavoured milk to 5 lakh children from 14 talukas under the Doodh Sanjivani Yojana, etc.

- The Mahatma Gandhi Cleanliness Campaign and its activities were largely an important social initiative that brought to the fore Anandiben's urban development and planning vision. It included approving and facilitating solid and liquid waste management in 2,500 villages; beginning the campaign of providing extensive information through education and correspondence; distributing more than 75,000 tools and devices for the management of solid waste in 159 municipalities with a total cost of ₹100 crore; 100 per cent door-to-door collection of solid waste in 25 municipalities; providing medical check-ups for the staff of the municipal corporation and municipalities; planning to provide 50,000 personal toilet facilities and facilitating the approval for 85,000 new toilets, etc.
- Strengthening public service management was a POI that favoured the common man in the state and was aimed at fulfilling his expectation from a government that he had voted for. The action points included concluding 100 Lok Samwad Setu programmes in 100 days; organizing a Garib Kalyan Mela in every municipal corporation and municipality

areas; distributing forest title deeds to 5,000 vanbandhus; organizing a Karmayogi Chintan Shibir at the taluka and district levels; settling red tapism issues at the state, district and taluka levels; strengthening the SWAGAT online programme at the taluka level; connecting 51,000 non-resident Gujaratis (NRGs) with Gujarat; facilitating the Centre's nod to new city civic centres in 25 municipalities of the state, etc.

- Modernization of revenue records was a step towards realizing the ideal and modern Gujarat model of development and offered solutions to all pending registrations for inheritance; solutions to all the other pending registrations within 100 days; facilitated the organization of special camps for hereditary registration in tribal areas; arranged for the implementation of *Baki Kami Zasti Patrak* as a campaign in rural panchayats; provided solutions to transform old proviso cases to new provisos, etc.
- One POI was preparing a recruitment calendar to give employment a push and to ensure smoothly manned administration machinery. Under this, the Gujarat administration services class-1 and class-2 recruitments would happen through combined competitive examinations. Around 20,000 recruitments were targeted in the year 2014. A recruitment fair was POI aimed at providing knowledge regarding various employment avenues and securing jobs, and included the employment to 75,000 people through 347 employment-recruitment fairs within 100 days, and providing information regarding foreign employment at the Ahmedabad and Vadodara centres.

- Infrastructural facilities in Gujarat urban mission cities saw activities like implementing an underground drainage project worth ₹102 crore; starting the work to build 19 sewage treatment plants of 134 MLD capacity; and approving a pure drinking water project worth ₹230 crore.
- The Karmayogi Abhiyan Training and qualitative reform had a push in the direction of getting an electronic learning portal for government employees up and running; facilitating the preparation of 25 modules to provide training to government employees; implementing an action plan to train more than 35,000 employees of municipal corporations and municipalities under the programme.
- The Smart Learning programme in schools was a step towards achieving digital milestones in education, and included the implementation of e-learning in 500 smart schools and the organization of the Nirmal Shala Abhiyan across all the schools during the next 100 days.
- Another POI to upgrade skills that work as an advantage in helping the candidate get employment and to facilitate that training was imparted in 125 industrial training institutions (ITIs) in collaboration with the Industrial Kaushalya Vardhan Kendra (I-KVK). The I-KVK provides a skill certificate that signifies a unique recognition of the person's acquired skills, and can be beneficial in the future, when the candidate opts for a job. Short-term training classes were arranged to upgrade the development of multiple skills; candidates were prepared for campus placements in 50 nodals; around 25,000 workers were provided certifications based on their

work experience and hereditary skills; imparting training and distributing kits to 5,000 farmers who had claimed land rights under the Forest Authority Act under the Wadi Yojana.

As soon as the targets were set, the departments started to work in a fast-track mode to achieve the outlined goals. In her tenure as chief minister, Anandiben's focus and work on the Gatisheel Gujarat project wasn't the only highlight, but the first among many such initiatives. Anandiben went on to launch several schemes and campaigns for the benefit of the people. In her first few months in office, she showed the entire county what transformation means and how it can be brought about at all levels, be it at the grassroots or higher up—her aim was the overall development of Gujarat.

She conducted a review after the first 100 days to check progress, and followed it up with another review after six months. Follow-ups were a regular practice.

Anandiben continued to focus on children and women through various schemes. Her dynamic thinking came to the fore through another noble initiative that helped implement the Maa Vatsalya Yojana scheme. There were many families who did not fall under any 'extreme' category to be able to claim benefits from prevalent government schemes. Anandiben often received complaints from people who were neither privileged nor very poor and thus could not avail any scheme. Such families did not have any special cards—a classic case of the neglected lower- and middle-class strata of society.

Anandiben launched the MA Vatsalya Yojana after much discussion with her officers to make sure that this segment of the population benefited. Through this yojana, lower- and middle-income groups were given a free health insurance card worth ₹200,000. The card had to be renewed every year and was reissued on the basis of income slab.

Having grown up in a farmer's family, Anandiben was aware of the problems a farmer faces. There are times when natural calamities lead to farmers losing their crops, and all their efforts to salvage anything are in vain. A farmer's earnings are dependent on the yearly growth of crops. Anandiben had seen how droughts and excessive rain could spoil a whole year's hard work. Just like any other occupation, even a farmer requires financial support for various agricultural needs. At the time, many banks issued loans at 18 per cent interest rate to the farmers and most failed to repay them. Anandiben's predecessor, Modi, had made finding solutions to the farmers' problems a priority. When she took over, she carried the same vision forward. She implemented many policies where farmers were able to buy equipment, fertilizers and other things at a much lower rate. The bank loan's interest rate was reduced to 1 per cent from 8 per cent for the farmers. However, Anandiben wanted it to be 0 per cent because she knew what it meant to be a farmer, but that was not a possible outcome.

She also accelerated the construction work of the Narmada Canal; she procured the remaining land and got the canal network completed.

With Modi at the helm as the prime minister, instant approval was facilitated for the Sardar Sarovar Dam gate. Anandiben made sure that farmers did not suffer any loss; rather, she gave them multiple benefits. Farming was in her blood and it was her prime duty to take care of the farmers. She even gave land to women who were involved in the dairy business. She provided machines and safe shelters for free. These steps made all the farmers and their families in the state feel happy and secure.

As the campaign Gatisheel Gujarat completed its first 100 days, Anandiben called for another high-level meeting to address the collectors, district development officers and superintendents of police to review the progress of the campaign in 12 districts of the Saurashtra region in Rajkot. She also called for coordination among the departments. She asked the officers to take the lead in creating awareness and implementing the government's welfare projects, such as nutritious food for extremely malnourished children and iron-enriched food for lactating mothers. To check crime against women, Anandiben called for adequate publicity and promotion to ensure greater participation of women in lok darbars held at police stations.

She also asked the administration to proactively implement cleanliness at hospitals, health centres and public places. She made sure that the in-house toilet campaign was taken up on mission mode as corporate social responsibility, in collaboration with industrial houses and voluntary organizations, taking people from all walks of life, in a time-bound manner. She called for the need to provide training to job aspirants at the district level to participate in competitive examinations. Anandiben wanted to create effective public awareness about the campaign.

The campaign had been rolled out, and now it was time to check the results. Anandiben called for a meeting that was attended by Chief Secretary D.J. Pandian, Additional Chief Secretary G.R. Aloria and M.S. Dagur, principal secretaries and secretaries, and municipal commissioners. She asked all the concerned officials of the district and cities to display the progress of Gatisheel Gujarat, and the unique identities and icons of their respective areas through attractive hoardings, banners and boards at prime locations to create a new image. She communicated to the officials the urgent need to fulfil the targets of various people's welfare programmes. At the same time, the administration had to maintain a progressive attitude to ensure that the changes in the lifestyle of the common man were appreciated.

The meeting reviewed the progress of rural development agencies in constructing individual toilets, roads and buildings, health, women and child welfare, housing under the Sardar Awas Yojana, revenue, police and other departments. Anandiben drilled the need to monitor progress, measure results and use them to spread further awareness about the 100 Days campaign.

Anandiben wanted to see the anganwadi workers, members of the self-help groups and Asha workers to ask them to work as ground agents for change. Under the Gatisheel Gujarat initiative, the administration spread information about various central schemes as well, such as the Sukanya Nidhi Yojana, Pradhan Mantri Mudra Yojana, and skill development and bank loan facilities to reach job seekers and entrepreneurs through publicity and promotion.

During this time, Anandiben met her ex-colleague and best friend from her teaching days, Meenakshiben. As the old friends spoke, Anandiben became aware of the poor condition of women who suffer from cancer. She came to know that many women who were suffering from cancer were either unaware of the severity of their condition or not financially sound enough to get appropriate treatment.

In keeping with her solution-oriented thinking, Anandiben promptly organized a system to address the issue. She arranged for free health check-ups and treatment for women suffering from breast or cervical cancer. All the community health centres (CHCs) were instructed to do a survey and organize health camps to identify and support such women. Within a few months, more than 1,500 women were examined and treated for cancer. Anandiben believes that a woman is the backbone of a family, and if something happens to her, the entire family collapses. She upheld that taking care of our mothers, sisters and daughters was our prime responsibility. This particular initiative of Anandiben endeared her, especially to the people of Gujarat, who still remember her as their life saviour.

In the field of health, Anandiben set another example by setting up the Kidney Transplant University. Dr H.L. Trivedi, a renowned surgeon from the US, had returned to India to serve the nation. He had always wanted to use his knowledge and experience from many years of research and practice for his countrymen. He and his wife started their work in the kidney hospital of Ahmedabad. He was praised across the globe for his service and expertise in kidney transplants. At his meeting with Anandiben, he told her that he wanted to convert the hospital into a university. 'I thought about his idea and decided that there should be a university for kidney and liver transplants,' Anandiben remembers how this suggestion pushed her to act on it. She had the Bill passed in Vidhan Sabha and soon, a separate building for the university was erected.

Anandiben inaugurated the university by laying the foundation stone. As the inauguration commenced, Dr Trivedi had tears in his eyes. He had never seen a politician think and act so quickly.

He told Anandiben that the purpose of his life had been fulfilled with her valuable support. Many citizens did and still continue to benefit from the university.

In Anandiben's tenure, many six- and four-lane roads were constructed. Her vision was to create wider roads so that people did not face difficulties in travelling. This was also the time when she became aware of the corruption and violence at road toll centres. They often led to heavy traffic jams and impeded smooth communication. Anandiben declared that all light-weight vehicles were to be exempted from paying toll tax. The government decided to pay it on behalf of the people. Gujarat became the first state to establish a free toll-tax network.

Anandiben was a role model for women in politics in the state of Gujarat. The elevation of Anandiben galvanized the BJP women's wing. In her rallies, supporters raised the slogan: '*Nari shakti, zindabad* (Hail, women power)!' She had carved out a place for herself as a strong leader among women. Ironically, however, the percentage of women contesting elections in the state was very low. Unless women candidates had political connections or a rich background, they were not given tickets. It was difficult for common women to be a part of politics. Now Anandiben knew the struggle first-hand, of course, she had risen to the top, but it had taken years of working from the ground up and that work being recognized by senior leaders. She resolved to provide help in this struggle. She had observed, during her time as the president of the Mahila Morcha, that many families did not allow their women to participate in politics and she vowed to change this.

After 33 per cent reservation for women, many of them got

jobs. Anandiben had worked in various capacities for the past 10 years towards the improvement of the conditions of women living in villages. The Bill for providing 50 per cent reservations to women was still pending for the last four years, but as soon as Anandiben became the chief minister, she pushed for it and passed the bill with the support of high court judges, in 2015.

Thus, respect for Anandiben increased among Gujarati women. They had never seen a leader who thought as much about women empowerment as Anandiben had right from the start. Following the Bill, many women were able to grow professionally. This brought about a deep social change and people understood the power of women. From safety to security, women in Gujarat had it all.

After completing one year in governance as the chief minister, Anandiben wrote a blog detailing how her inclusive and sustainable development effort was a huge success. She wrote,

> I took charge as the CM (Chief Minister), when there was a 90-day code of conduct (due to Lok Sabha polls) across the state, which had stalled many development works. There was a need to bring the administration back on track, with time-bound target achievement and that is when I sowed the seeds of the Gatisheel Gujarat campaign, for Gujarat's inclusive and sustainable development. It began with a 100-day target and then as a 150-day target. These campaigns were a huge success and fully served their purpose. Now, this campaign has become an institutionalized mechanism for the state to grow and prosper. More than just a mechanism, today, Gatisheel Gujarat has become a new identity of our state;

> enhancing the momentum in the direction carved out by Narendrabhai (Prime Minister Narendra Modi) during the past thirteen years. The past one year is just a milestone in this journey and you all, we all, are together in this! During this one year, many initiatives, decisions, announcements, policies took shape in Gujarat covering varied sectors and people from all strata of society.[15]

She also wrote that her achievement of making women fearless, instilling confidence in youth and empowering farmers satisfied her the most.

During her days in office, Anandiben documented her journey of governing Gujarat through many such blog posts. Anandiben addressed her countrymen through her writings. She expressed that both she and Gujarat were privileged to have hosted the twin high-profile events in January 2015. The state was filled with national and international delegates and visitors. In addition, the annual International Kite Festival added more vibrancy to the festive atmosphere in the state.

The international events were celebrating iconic milestones that year. First, Gujarat was chosen to host the Pravasi Bharatiya Divas to mark the centenary year of Gandhiji's return to India from South Africa; and second, the Vibrant Gujarat Summit basked in the glory of the world recognizing a new India since May 2014. With eight country partners, more than 25,000 delegates from 120

---

[15]PTI, '"Gatisheel Gujarat" Has Been a Success, Claims Gujarat CM Anandiben', *The Economic Times*, 22 May 2015, https://bit.ly/3Arr4Q4. Accessed on 26 August 2022.

countries, chief executive officers (CEOs) from more than 300 leading companies, the scale of the summit was much bigger than what it had been in the past. In Anandiben's own words, 'For me it became all the more special as it was the first summit as chief minister of Gujarat.'[16]

Anandiben remembers that the most defining moment during the entire summit was to see dignitaries from the world over, speaking the language of Gujarat. When Mr Ban Ki-Moon, secretary general of the United Nations, addressed the congregation with *'Kem chho? Tamne maline anand thayo!* (How are you? It was nice meeting you)', it felt as if the determination to scale new avenues of development had got the world talking their language.

She wrote, 'Today, when I sit back and think of it, I feel extremely blessed to have got the opportunity to be able to host such a grand event.' There were so many nitty-gritties involved in the run-up to the event that working on them kept her and the state machinery completely engrossed. Even one small thing going wrong would have led to chaos but it all happened with clockwork precision. She added, 'I do not have any words to thank the Almighty for granting us such a great success. It would have not been possible without divine grace.'

She acknowledged the hard work of every single contributor and wrote,

> I thank everyone right from the Union Ministers to my Cabinet colleagues, Team Gujarat, and the citizens of Gujarat for the success

[16]'Chief Minister Smt. Anandiben Patel's blog: On the Shoulders of Giants', *Desh Gujarat*, 20 January 2015, https://bit.ly/3vRKR9E. Accessed on 9 August 2022.

> of these high-profile events. I also thank the media for beautifully covering both the events that boosted the image of Gujarat being a competent state. The hard work of numerous people paid off.[17]

In hindsight, Anandiben found two noteworthy things about these events. First, it was the coming together of all Indians residing in different parts of the world to Gujarat to mark the centenary of the return of Gujarat's great son Mahatma Gandhi to his soil. Second, for centuries the Gujarati people had been going overseas for business and now the global business community was converging under the home roof of Vibrant Gujarat. To her, it felt like the entire wheel of time had come full circle.

The Vibrant Gujarat Summit marked the beginning of a new chapter of progress, prosperity and peace for India and the world. An atmosphere of new hope, a new awakening, which she felt was captured beautifully by a poet in the following verses:

> કાલચક્રની વીધી કાલિમા
> ઉજાસને અવ નહી કોઈ સીમા
> જ્યોતિઆજે પ્રગટી ઊઠી
> જાણે નવ&રંગી પરવાળાઅજવાળાં અજવાળાં આજે અજવાળાં અજવાળાં
> Crossing the darkness of time,
> The light has lit today,
> Bringing boundless glow all around.
> Like nine-coloured coral-lit lights.

Anandiben hoped that in the days to come, the state would continue to progress with the aim and vision of a 'smart state'. Gujarat had

[17]Ibid.

created a unique identity for itself among all the states of India. The whole country and the world had its eye set on the next step that Gujarat would take. She mentioned a popular saying which stated, if I have seen further, it is by standing on the shoulders of giants.

These giants were Gujarat's great sons: Gandhi, Sardar Patel and, now, Narendra Modi, who had been a beacon in the state's exemplary success. It was the vision and leadership of these giants that had helped the state and its citizens carve a niche for itself. In her own words, 'I feel extremely fortunate of being the chief minister of a progressive state that stands on the shoulders of such giants. I call on each and every Gujarati to optimize on the strong foundation we have by supporting the state government's endeavour to put Gujarat in line with developed countries of the world.'[18]

The verses that Anandiben had cited were written by none other than the architect of this vibrant Gujarat, Modi. Those verses are from his book, *Aankh aa Dhanya che* (Blessed are My Eyes) (Image Publications, 2007), and the title of the poem is 'Aash' (Hope).

The state that was the source of so much of her pride, in turn, owed a lot to Anandiben as well. Many considered that she was one of the giants on whose shoulders the state and its vision had leapfrogged. In her various capacities and roles, she had done untiring work to make the state grow stronger and benefit its citizens.

The Gujarat Public Service Commission (GPSC) also gained strength under Anandiben's leadership. The GPSC focused on matters relating to methods of recruitment to various administrative services in the state. In close consultation with Dinesh Das, then

---

[18]Ibid.

the chairman of the GPSC, she suggested creating a yearly calendar. A comprehensive schedule covering examinations in the upcoming years was prepared so that the aspirants knew about the examinations and results. Unique IDs were assigned, date sheets were uploaded and a transparent system was created. The portal started posting new opportunities and knowledge material. Today, the GPSC holds examinations, and provides scanned optical mark recognition (OMR) answer sheets and digital assessment.

The twenty-first-century global pandemic almost paralysed the world and showed the glaring loopholes in healthcare management in the modern era. People suffered as basic equipment like ventilators and personal protective equipment (PPE) kits ran out of stock. Scientists all around the world struggled to find vaccines, and healthcare systems started collapsing. It proved the importance of focusing on the healthcare system for a leader. Back in 2015, Anandiben had started the first health university in Gujarat. The university was the first of its kind in the country. It was set up to inform people about diseases and prevention of the same. The university gave health education to youth and women and provided training to government officers for situations like natural disasters or epidemics. The country could really gain by following this university model, where people and authorities alike gain knowledge about healthcare management.

In 2005, the forest department under Modi's leadership developed several acres of land by planting trees to create a unique botanical garden with astrological significance in keeping with mythology. Puneet Van in Gandhinagar inspired Anandiben's initiatives and thoughts to protect nature. She established four more such forest areas. The former minister in charge of urban development and planning was now implementing this action to increase the number of trees in the state and create a balance of nature with urbanization.

In schools, Anandiben introduced the Student Police Cadet, or SSP, programmes. She was a teacher and she knew it was really important to provide value and physical education to the students. The students were selected and trained over the weekends for the programme. SSP students performed on Independence Day and Republic Day parades, which boosted their confidence to serve the nation. Eventually, SSP students started participating in many government events, which gave them further exposure. The SSP programme created its identity in many schools across the state. It was demanded that SSP should be introduced in all the schools, and, thus, the comprehensive process began. The programme instilled values of service and compassion towards society. Within a few months, officers from the Border Security Force (BSF) started training SSP students and many were given uniforms. This really motivated the students to learn and work for the country.

An interesting, and at the same time amazing, thing to notice about Anandiben was that she always carried a small notepad and pen with her. Wherever she travelled, she noted down the issues and requirements of the area. When she was in charge of the roads and buildings department of the state, she made a note of the roads that needed attention in the villages she visited. She noticed all the bridges, community centres, etc., and immediately assigned grants wherever required. In 2015, she allocated a budget of around ₹10,000 crore to finish the pending projects of rural development. She took part in all the meetings from planning to budget estimation. With this budget, many villages in Gujarat received new roads, bridges and canals. This not only benefited the residents but also the hospitals and schools in rural areas.

Soon, Anandiben completed one year as the chief minister of Gujarat. One year of offering her sweat and blood to the state. She expressed all her attendant emotions of heading the state through another blog post for the people.

Her post started with a reminiscence of the eventful date of 22 May a year ago, when she was given the privilege of serving her people as the chief minister. Anandiben narrated that her year-long journey's most satisfying glimpses were that of fearlessness in the eyes of women, confidence among the youth and empowerment of farmers.

For a woman who was the driving force behind most of the monumental developments of the state, she never tired of thanking everyone for both their contribution and support. Anandiben always believed that growth was a united effort, and it is seen in her endeavours and projects, where she has always included the common man as well as the government officials. She reinforced her commitment in her blog address of wanting to reach her goal of putting a smile on every face.

Anandiben also talked about the 90-day-long code of conduct across the state prevalent during the beginning of her term. It had stalled many projects and the need of the hour was to bring the administration back to momentum with time-bound target achievement. She pointed out how that was when the seeds of 'Gatisheel Gujarat' were sown. First with a 100-Day target and then with a target of 150 days that focused on Gujarat's inclusive and sustainable development, the campaigns successfully served their purpose. With the launch of the third edition with year-long targets, the campaign had become an institutionalized mechanism for the state.

She was proud that her ideation of Gatisheel Gujarat had become the new identity of the state, consistent with Modi's vision. Anandiben considered that her first anniversary was just a milestone where many initiatives, decisions, announcements and policies took shape in Gujarat, covering varied sectors and people from all strata of society. The government and her motto behind each step had been, 'All for one, one for all'. She constantly asked for the support of the people and assured them of her persistence in delivering all government schemes.

Anandiben's dream for her state to be self-reliant can be gauged from the last lines of her post. 'It is said that for a region to develop well, either the administrative machinery has to be aware, agile and adept, or the citizens. Just imagine what will happen if both the administration and the people have these virtues!'[19]

During her tenure, she had made one thing very clear to her children: to not ask for any favours in her name. This was the level of discipline in her house. Also, because of Anandiben's straight way of dealing with people or matters and her honest nature, there was no danger to her family from any quarter. Her family did not cheat or defame anyone. She never had enemies and was never scared. She reiterates that one is afraid only when they do wrong.

---

[19]'Anandiben Patel Blogs on One Year of Her Government in Gujarat', *Desh Gujarat*, 22 May 2015, https://bit.ly/3Ti8jqG. Accessed on 26 August 2022.

A Series of Protests

A 'No' uttered from the deepest conviction is better than a 'Yes' merely uttered to please, or worse, to avoid trouble.

—Mahatma Gandhi

Anandiben was highly respected in the state for her vision and commitment towards work. She was popularly recognized as Ben. After a year of her governance, the local residents of the state were often heard saying, '*Jo tamne koi samasya chhe, toh Ben teno hala karashe* (If you have any problem, Ben will solve it).'

Anandiben was like a big sister to more than six crore Gujaratis. She had dedicated her life to the people of Gujarat. Plans for transforming the state and thoughts about its future ran through its first woman chief minister's head day and night. She motivated many women to be courageous and step up to work for the country. She became an example for them. She proved that nothing was impossible if you followed your mission with honesty and hard work. Many women from the villages appeared in civil service examinations, many joined the defence forces and many went for higher education, following in the footsteps of their leader.

Unfortunately, things took a political downturn in 2015 for Anandiben. While she was envisioning a progressive and inclusive Gujarat, she faced one of the biggest protests the country had ever seen. Still, it was her grit and discipline that helped her face every bit of it.

In July 2015, the people of the Patidar community, seeking reservation status for Other Backward Classes (OBC), held public demonstrations across the state of Gujarat. Anandiben came to know about the protests through Lalji Patel in Mehsana. When she asked Nitin Patel about the intensity of the protests and the people involved, she received a report stating that it was being held by a very small section of people with unrealistic demands. Anandiben, being a Patidar leader and chief minister of the state, was expected to bow down and accept the request.

Around the same time, the Patidar agitation started in Mansa on 22 July. In no time, the protest grew and was joined by a popular youth Patidar leader, Hardik Patel. The very next day, on 23 July, a demonstration held in Visnagar turned violent with arson and vandalization of public vehicles and the office of MLA Rishikesh Patel. There was no action taken by the MLA and other local authorities. This encouraged the protestors.

Soon, demonstrations were also held in Vijapur and Mehsana on 28 July. The police arrested more than 150 people for violating government orders and holding these demonstrations. Anandiben promptly called for a meeting to address the series of protests in the state. She was concerned about the people who were getting affected. She asked the law-and-order authorities to take control of the situation, rein in the rioters and maintain peace in the state.

In India, the OBC status provides reserved quotas in education and government jobs. In Gujarat, 27 per cent of the seats in government and education are reserved for the OBCs, 7.5 per cent for the Scheduled Castes and 15 per cent for the Scheduled Tribes, forming a total of 49.5 per cent of all seats. The Supreme Court in 1992 had capped the reservation percentage at 50 per cent following the Indra Sawhney case.

In 1981, the government of Gujarat, headed by the Congress chief minister, Madhavsinh Solanki, introduced reservation for socially and economically backward castes (SEBC, which later became OBC) based on recommendations of the Bakshi Commission. This was followed by anti-reservation agitation across the state that soon turned violent and claimed more than a hundred lives. While Solanki resigned in 1985, he returned to power again with the support of Kshatriya, Harijan, Adivasi and Muslims, collectively called KHAM. Other communities, including Patidars, as a result, lost most of their political influence. The Patidars represent 12.3 per cent of the population of Gujarat.

As the OBC reservation list grew from 81 communities to 146 by 2014, the Patidar community complained of facing class differentiation within the community. The Patidar youth perceived shrinking economic opportunities and the older generation, a downward social mobility. Slowly, this discontent grew like a forest fire in Gujarat. Taking their cue from the Gujjar agitation in Rajasthan that concluded in May 2015, the Patidars, mostly with

Patel as their last name, launched theirs in July 2015, demanding OBC reservation status.

Hardik Patel became the leader of the Patidar Anamat Andolan Samiti (PAAS), formed with the support of Sardar Patel Sevadal, a community service organization. Notably, though, there were four major Patidar organizations who took no part in the agitation. Later, the Khodaldham Trust offered to negotiate mediation between the youth and the government.

Before Anandiben could comprehend and plan the resolution of the Patidar community's protest across the nation, another unfortunate and horrific incident took place in Una (Unnatnagar), a city and a municipality in Gir Somnath district of the Saurashtra region. On 11 July 2016, a video showing the assault of seven Dalit family members on the pretext of protesting cow slaughter shocked the state. They were approached by some gaurakshaks in two cars who accused them of killing cows. Although the Dalits explained that the carcasses had been bought at Bediya village, they were tied to the car and beaten mercilessly. They were then taken to Una where they were stripped and assaulted in public. When the police arrived, the attackers fled. The Dalits had to be taken to the hospital.

As social media fanned the widespread circulation of the video, more and more protests took the state by storm. Gujarat saw the first huge protest on 12 July in Chandkheda, Ahmedabad, which was attended by 2,000 Dalits and their leaders, who blocked the state highway. The next day, hundreds of Dalits held a protest rally in Trikon Baug, the main square in Una, for an hour. On 21 July, the issue was discussed in Rajya Sabha, the Upper House of Parliament. The protests continued to spread across the Saurashtra region. In one of the protests, 12 Dalit youth attempted suicide publicly, and one of them died. Several dozen were injured when efforts were on to rescue the youths. This number included seven police personnel and bystanders.[20]

The Dalit Asmita Yatra from Ahmedabad to Una brought to the fore activist Jignesh Mevani. Apart from justice, he demanded land from the government for the upliftment of these communities. The protest ended on 15 August and was attended by some 20,000 Dalits who pledged to give up cow carcass collection—their traditional vocation. These protests also saw backlash as participants were attacked and vehicles torched on their way back from their 10-day *azadi kooch* (freedom march).[21]

Anandiben visited the Mota Samadhiyala village to understand the situation better. She reached the village where she consoled the affected families and also promised that the victims would be given support from the state government.

By then, the government had filed almost 74 cases against the protesters for disrupting law and order.[22] The victims were not pacified by Anandiben's visit and started a hunger strike against the government. They sought mercy killing for themselves as they did not expect the government to fulfil the promises. Violent protests

---

[20]PTI, 'Attack on Dalits: 7 More Youth Attempt Suicide amid Protests in Gujarat', *The Asian Age*, 21 July 2016, https://bit.ly/3Qa6M41. Accessed on 9 August 2022.
[21]Maanvi, 'In Pics: 10-day Azaadi Kooch Dalit March to Una Is on Its Way', *The Quint,* 6 August 2016, https://bit.ly/3Aa1yzY. Accessed on 9 August 2022.
[22]'Una Dalit Victims Seek Mercy Killing, Write to President, Say "Government Didn't Fulfill Promises"', *The Indian Express*, 28 November 2018, https://bit.ly/3zKllUV. Accessed on 9 August 2022.

continued in Saurashtra and north Gujarat, where arson, blockade, clashes and attempted suicides were widely reported. The authorities resorted to shutdowns and use of force by police to restore order.

The fact-finding committee led by Kaushik Parmar stated that the upsurge created by beating up Dalits skinning a cow was not an isolated incident. Cow protection committees had been harassing Dalits often in the past months.[23] After the Patidar protests, this was yet another issue facing Anandiben. She wanted to control the situation in a peaceful manner to avoid any harm to the local citizens and without exacerbating the circumstances.

The social media furore, however, was relentless and encouraged the spread of the Patidar and Dalit protests quickly across the state. Demonstrations were held in Devbhoomi Dwarka, Gandhinagar, Navsari, Jam Jodhpur, Himmatnagar and Bagasara districts.

Anandiben formed a seven-member panel headed by Nitinbhai Patel, and included Ramanlal Vora, Bhupendrasinh Chudasama, Babubhai Bokhiria, Vasuben Trivedi, Nanubhai Vanani and Rajnikant Patel. The panel was asked to interact with the Patidar community and to submit a report to the government.

The protestors, though, were enjoying coverage in the media and avoided meetings or any attempt at a peaceful conclusion to the violence. The panel tried to interact with Hardik Patel but he put up a condition that along with the panel, the chief minister, too, had to be present at all the meetings. These attempts at derailing negotiations, including not showing up for meetings,

---

[23]PTI, 'For Cow Vigilantes, Dalits Are Soft Target: Fact Finding Team', NDTV, 21 July 2016, https://bit.ly/3bKeAuj. Accessed on 9 August 2022.

distracted the people and prevented a solution being reached. All this led to continued protests and Hardik Patel's wilful neglect of talks allowed the discontent to spread further in the state, disturbing its peace.

On 17 August, the city of Surat came to a standstill as diamond and textile markets, schools and colleges were closed in anticipation of a demonstration that drew crowds estimated at 4 lakh people. Similar demonstrations were held in Surendranagar, Bharuch, Ankleshwar and Vadodara on 21 August. The state witnessed a total of 149 protest rallies within 55 days.

This was a trying time for Anandiben, who had to shift her focus from development to the unrest. Still, she was clear that she would not give in to the demand of providing reservation to the Patidars. She was in favour of reservation but only when done on the basis of economic background. Anandiben said that the Patidars are a community of people who help others. They feed the villagers. This is what she expected out of the Patidars—their support, not protests. She was upset that people who were well-to-do were fighting for something like reservation. They did not understand their own capabilities.

The demonstration, dubbed Kranti Rally, was attended by over 5 lakh protesters. A memorandum of demands was prepared and Hardik Patel insisted that it had to be received by the chief minister. He threatened to go on hunger strike unto death, if not.

This was blackmail, plain and simple. Anandiben had no intention of visiting the protest site and encouraging their insensitive demands. She was clear on her stand while others were busy doing politics and gaining benefits out of the outrage. There was a lot of pressure

Anandiben Patel with Rajnath Singh, the now defense minister of India

Anandiben Patel with elder sister Saritaben

Anandiben Patel with sisters

Anandiben cooking on chulha with family

At a Mahila Samelan meet, Mehsana, Gujarat, 2007

Oath-taking ceremony as Cabinet Minister, 2008

Review meeting, Patan Constituency, Gujarat, 2012

At the Gandhinagar Lok Sabha election rally with Atal Bihari Vajpayee

Swearing in as Cabinet Minister, 26 December 2012

During Gunotsav at a government primary school , 2013

Anandiben Patel elected as the leader of the party, Gandhinagar, Gujarat, 21 May 2014

Narendra Modi's farewell at the Gujarat Vidhan Sabha, 21 May 2014

Oath-taking ceremony for the office of chief minister, Gandhinagar, Gujarat, 22 May 2014

Anandiben Patel with Narendra Modi and her Cabinet Ministers at Raj Bhavan, Gandhinagar, Gujarat, 2014

Taking Saritaben's blessings before becoming chief minister

First file signed as chief minister

Reviewing SWAGAT online programme, 2014

Promoting health and nourishment in schools as chief minister

Anandiben with daughter Anar Patel and son-in-law Jayesh Patel

Anandiben with son Swetank, daughter-in-law Heena and grandson Dharma

Oath-taking ceremony as governor of Madhya Pradesh

Anandiben meeting the children of an anathashram (orphanage) after taking oath as governor of Madhya Pradesh, 23 January 18

Anandiben in the Madhya Pradesh governor's office

World Book of Records award being presented to Anandiben for conducting the largest book-reading programme, Bhopal, Madhya Pradesh, 2018

Anandiben marching as a part of the oath-taking ceremony in Lucknow Raj Bhavan

Anandiben taking oath as Governor of Uttar Pradesh

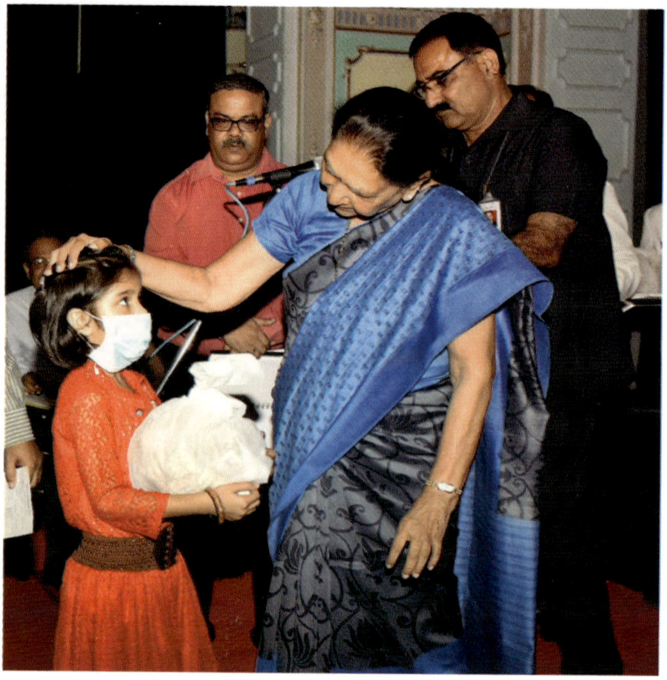

Anandiben adopted a girl child suffering from tuberculosis at the TB Mukt Uttar Pradesh event

Anandiben conducting a school inspection in Lucknow

from the media and the Opposition on Anandiben to meet the protestors.

Anandiben declared, '*Jo a babata sambandhita nathi, to hum tyam ja isa nahim. Anyatha te one protsahita karavamam avase* (If the matter is not relevant, I will not visit anywhere. Otherwise, it will encourage the protestors).' She went to Una instead, to provide relief and extend a helping hand to the affected Dalit families. Meanwhile, there was a lot of speculation at the Cabinet level. The Centre had started to take notice of the entire issue and was poised to intervene. Suddenly, everything came undone at once.

An arrest warrant was issued against Hardik Patel, citing his lack of permission to be present on the grounds after the rally. Since arresting the leader led to a commotion among his followers, the police had to resort to heavy force to disperse the crowd. Anandiben had not been kept in the loop on this and it came as a shock to her. She was agitated with the authorities for taking that step without consultation, but the damage had been done. An inquiry was ordered to probe the use of police force.

Both the state leaders, Anandiben Patel and Home Minister Rajnikant Patel, denied ordering or authorizing the police charge at the crowd. Right on cue, some days later, Hardik Patel was released and all of it looked like a carefully staged drama. This was followed by more incidents of violence, clashes, arson and vandalization, all in the name of reservation for a particular community. The loss of property and causing harm to the state and its people had stopped being a concern.

The Patidar agitation was considered a blot on Anandiben's otherwise stellar performance. On the other end, she looked at it as some kind of betrayal. She was all alone, misinformed and misguided. She tried to connect the dots and take control of the chaos, but things had already gone out of hand.

Clashes were being reported between the Rabaris and Patels in Ghatlodiya. Railway tracks and vehicles were being damaged, and police and media personnel were being attacked. The Ahmedabad Municipal Corporation suffered damages worth ₹12 crore that included vandalization of public transport, ward offices and civic centres.[24] The city was put under curfew and the army was deployed to control the situation.

The city of Surat, too, faced a curfew as the mob torched buses, ATMs, the fire station and vehicles on the streets and also damaged property. The Ahmedabad Vadodara Expressway was blocked by agitators and damage to buses led to the cancellation of 1,554 bus trips.[25] The trouble to the common man can only be imagined as they were the ones who suffered the repercussions. The damage to public and private property by violent mobs in Rajkot was estimated at ₹1.47 crore.

Curfew was also imposed in Visnagar and Unjha of Mehsana, Morbi, Amreli and Patan. The house of Home Minister Rajnikant Patel was torched, among many other mindless acts of vandalism. The police made a few arrests but nothing could control the violence.

Following the attack on her Cabinet Minister's house, Anandiben

---

[24]'Patidar Andolan: AMC Suffers Rs 12 Crore Damages in Public Properties', *Desh Gujarat*, 30 August 2015, https://bit.ly/3bIqIfy. Accessed on 9 August 2022.

[25]TNN, 'Patel Agitation for OBC Quota: GSRTC Cancels 1,554 Bus Trips', *The Times of India*, 27 August 2015, https://bit.ly/3BRFrPT. Accessed on 9 August 2022.

sat in her office looking at the reports of violence. It was 2.00 a.m., but her beloved Gujarat was burning and the people who had put her in the highest seat of state governance deserved answers and solutions. She thought about what could stop the riots. She asked herself if the government should accept the demands, or should she stand for what was right.

Anandiben has always done what was right regardless of the consequences, both in her professional and personal life. Standing with what was right comes at a cost and she has been paying it since the day she joined politics. Her values and commitment to her nation were so strong that there was no compromising her ideals. She tried to resolve the matter amicably but clearly, there was a bigger political agenda at work than the protest, and she could not put the sanctity of truth at stake at any cost. She never had and never would.

The government deployed 3,500 paramilitary force personnel and 93 companies of the state reserve police. The agitation had cost the lives of 20 and led to the arrest of almost 700 people across districts.[26] The government blocked access to internet services on mobile phones, and certain newspapers and platforms like WhatsApp and Facebook in the state for six days from 26 to 31 August. According to Western Railways, damage to the tracks by the mobs led to the cancellation of 51 trains and affected the operation of 26, while 16 were diverted out of the state. The state-owned transport service GSRTC lost 140 buses to fire and 152 to damage. The

---

[26]TNN, 'Gujarat Violence Claims 9 Lives, State Govt Seeks Army Help', *The Times of India*, 27 August 2015, https://bit.ly/3JFZbYx. Accessed on 9 August 2022.

police department alone suffered damages worth ₹200 crore.[27]

The state limped back to normalcy by 28 August. Hardik Patel, however, declared his intention of expanding the agitation to the other state communities where he received support from groups, such as Jat, Kurmi and Gujjar organizations. The call for the campaign to petition the prime minister fizzled out eventually. Nonetheless, Hardik Patel launched a new organization on 9 September called the Patel Navnirman Sena (PNS) for nationwide extension of the agitation.

The government pressed for talks and Hardik Patel relented this time around. He met former chief minister, Keshubhai Patel, prior to a meeting with government members on 14 September. The second meeting was chaired by Anandiben and attended by all the Cabinet Ministers, where Hardik Patel and Lalji Patel along with 20 Patidar representatives were in attendance. The issues discussed included the police action on 25 August, scholarship schemes for general category students, compensation for people who had died in the violence and release of arrested people. However, the Patidars denied all the offers and were stuck at 10 per cent reservation. After the meeting, PAAS announced a march that would track the reverse route of the historic 1930 salt march from Dandi to Ahmedabad. All the heads of the 33 villages on the route to Dandi opposed the march and the Navsari district collector denied permission for it. The march was rescheduled to 13 September and, finally, called off.

On the other hand, to ease the situation, Anandiben announced offers of scholarships and subsidies to general category students on

[27]Ibid.

24 September 2015. The Patidars still remained adamant about their demands and Hardik Patel announced rallies in Madhya Pradesh and Bihar while the latter was counting days to the Legislative Assembly elections.

After the failed reverse Dandi rally, Hardik Patel organized the Ekta Yatra on 19 September in Varachha, Surat, but was detained along with 35 of his supporters. The authorities cited lack of permission and defying police notification as reasons. They were released on bail later but incidents of protests, arson, property damage and roadblocks in several cities and towns were reported. Once again, internet on mobile phones, social media and SMS services were blocked for a day in the affected parts. The government promptly deployed 12 companies each of the Border Security Force (BSF) and Rapid Action Force (RAF) to bring the violence under control.

On 24 September, Anandiben announced the Mukhyamantri Yuva Swavalamban Yojana or the Chief Minister's Youth Self-Reliance Scheme, offering scholarships and subsidies to general category students in higher education, and uniforms and free books in school education. She also offered age relaxation of five years in government jobs. The government also announced its intention to increase intake in medical and engineering education, and infrastructure such as student hostels. This was an obvious step to contain the Patidar agitation for OBC status and reservation benefits.

The package was announced at the end of the 10-day deadline set for the government to resolve the impasse during its 14 September meeting with the PAAS members. The implementation of the scheme was slated for the current academic year and cost the government ₹1,000 crore per year. The benefits of the scheme would reach at least 60,000 to 70,000 students who clear Class XII, in its first year.[28]

According to Hardik Patel, the scheme by Anandiben was just a 'lollipop' and did not meet their demands. He even launched a 'lollipop movement' to ridicule the step where he distributed lollipops to community members across the state. All of this did not affect Anandiben. She knew what she was doing, what the benefits of the scheme actually were, and for her, that was all that mattered.

The situation only worsened still. On 26 September, activist Umesh Patel from Rajkot died by suicide in support of the agitation. The state government ordered an inquiry into the case but the ball had been set in motion. As support poured in for the agitation from within and abroad, more and more organizations joined the protest, notable among them the Sardar Patel Seva Charitable Trust and the Umiya Mata Sansthan. Copycat protest fasts were launched and the authorities arrested nine persons from Himmatnagar but later released them on bail.

The deteriorating situation had Prime Minister Modi appealing for peace and resolution through dialogue. During the monsoon session of the Gujarat Legislative Assembly, the Opposition, namely the Congress, demanded a probe into the police atrocities following the 25 August rally. The assembly was suspended three times by the Speaker. All Congress MLAs, except opposition leader, Shankersinh Vaghela, were also suspended for a day.

---

[28]'Gujarat CM Announces Rs 1000 Crores Package for Students from EWS', *Gujarat Headline*, 25 September 2015, https://bit.ly/3bGPrkl. Accessed on 9 August 2022.

The Opposition saw the agitation as an opportunity to shake the hold of the BJP. On 1 October, Gurudas Kamat, general secretary of the Congress, announced its support for the agitation. The effect of the agitation was looming large on the upcoming local elections, in 2015. Nalin Kotdiya, BJP MLA from Dhari, Dipsinh Rathod, and Sabarkantha MP, declared their support for the agitation. Former chief minister of Gujarat, Madhav Singh Solanki, believed that the agitation would simmer down but Keshubhai Patel expressed his support towards the agitation as long as it remained non-violent. Amidst all this, Anandiben was thinking about the next steps to take. Apart from focusing on the protest, she had other important state tasks to look after.

Across the nation, opposition political parties blamed the Modi government for handling the protests with the use of force. Some even claimed that the agitation resulted from the BJP's 'politics of anger' as Rahul Gandhi termed it, and from a nationwide job scarcity.

Hardik Patel went on to address peasants and farmers at the Maha Kisan Panchayat as support came in from more quarters. Some Patidar community members protested the presence of politicians at garba venues during the Navratri festival in October. They also protested at functions attended by politicians. The agitation was again pointing towards a violent turn.

Hardik Patel threatened to stage a protest at the Saurashtra Cricket Association Stadium and to block the way of cricket players at the third One Day International cricket match between India and South Africa in Rajkot on 18 October 2015. It was a threat to the nation's image. When he was arrested along with six others, he stated that he had come to watch the match and nothing else.[29] Considering the earlier precedence of violence on his calls, the state government deployed heavy police presence and blocked internet services on the day. As expected, there were protests and rallies against Hardik's detention in Bardoli, Morbi, Surat and Tankara.

The spate of violence was worrying for the authorities in the face of upcoming local elections. The state government passed two ordinances to postpone the local governing body elections where the five-year terms ended in October–November 2015. These bodies included 253 municipalities, 208 taluka panchayats, 26 district panchayats and six municipal corporations. The ordinances were quashed by the Gujarat High Court as unconstitutional and directed the State Election Commission to hold the elections by December.

The police in Ahmedabad booked Hardik Patel and five other PAAS leaders under Indian Penal Code sections 121 (waging war against the government), 121A (using criminal force against the government), 124 (sedition), 153-A (promoting enmity between different communities), 120B (conspiracy) and 153-B (assertions prejudicial to national integrity). In Surat, Hardik Patel was booked under sedition charges for instigating a youth to kill policemen instead of committing suicide.

The next challenge for Anandiben and the party was to win the local civic elections in Gujarat. Anandiben was really concerned as many MLAs had backed off from campaigning. They were scared of being attacked by the protestors in their constituencies.

---

[29]PTI, 'Hardik Patel Threatens to Block India, South Africa Cricket Teams' Way to Rajkot Stadium', NDTV, 16 October 2015, https://bit.ly/3Pej7D0. Accessed on 9 August 2022.

Once again, Anandiben chose to lead by example. She called for an emergency meeting and declared that she would be going to the constituencies for campaigning. She said, *'Te maari pharaja che. Hun mari jaisha toh pana jaisha* (It's my duty. Even if I die, I will go).' She reiterated that the party was more important to her than her life. Many MLAs were motivated and joined her in campaigning. Anandiben decided to host campaign rallies in the cities. Because of the andolan, party workers were afraid to go to the villages. During Diwali, the high court gave orders to hold all the panchayat and municipality elections at the same time.

Anandiben recollects those days of campaigning in north Gujarat with interest. One such day, she was travelling in an open gypsy surrounded by her supporters. There was news that Patidar protestors would attack the rally but Anandiben decided to march ahead nonetheless. She did not change the routes or cancel the rally, rather, she said, 'It's OK if people want to express their anger. As a leader, we should have the capability to face both praise and criticism. If you are clear about your actions, nothing affects you.'

In Ahmedabad city, Anandiben started the initiative to start the election campaign. She would go to societies and be welcomed by hordes of people; she had earned their respect with her years of service to the people. This worked as an example for the workers. She then went to Surat, Rajkot, Jamnagar and Baroda. This resulted in the win in these cities.

As the caravan moved ahead in the streets of Visnagar, Anandiben came out in the open and waved at the supporters as they cheered and greeted, chanting her name. Suddenly, a stone came flying and, before Anandiben could comprehend what was happening, it hit her forehead. A mob raising slogans against Anandiben had merged into the crowd at some point. They were Patidar protestors. Anandiben got up and asked the party workers not to stop the rally. She moved ahead because she was committed, her forehead bleeding the entire time. 'It is okay. If I can take the praises, I am open to anger and criticism too. Let us move ahead!' she declared and the rally continued.

There were many party workers who supported Anandiben during the campaign. She mentions Mansukh L. Mandaviya in particular, who is now India's Union Minister for Health and Family Welfare. It was a tense time, as the local body polls were being considered a litmus test for the ruling BJP against the backdrop of the Patel quota agitation.

For local districts, she started with Patan. No leader was ready to join her. But she faced the people and their wrath. Then she did the whole round of north Gujarat. Most of the cities Anandiben visited were won by the BJP.

The elections were seen as a challenge for Chief Minister Anandiben Patel. These were also the first major polls in the state after she took over from Modi. The Congress was hoping to cash in on the resentment of the Patel community against the BJP. Several Patidar leaders urged voting against ruling BJP candidates and supporting Congress candidates. There was a lack of participation from many leaders within her party as well. The state Congress president Bharatsinh Solanki even hailed the election as a mini-election of sorts for the state and considered it as a verdict against the state government. According to the political secretary, Ahmed Patel, the ruling party had paid 'a heavy price for their vindictive attitude and witch hunt towards the (Patel) agitators'.[30]

Everyone underestimated Anandiben but she did not back away from holding the promotional campaigns for the party. She was attacked multiple times; her family, too, was under threat, but she went on to face the agitation. Anandiben gave her best effort to the party but she was not at peace due to the betrayals within the party. She waited for the election results.

The result day in December 2015 showed that the BJP suffered its worst loss in the local body elections in Gujarat in over a decade. The Congress gained lost ground, especially in rural areas. A clear divide was visible as the BJP managed to perform better in cities and towns due to the unstoppable efforts of Anandiben. In hindsight, this could be considered a blow for the BJP if we analyse it from the perspective of the 2017 state polls.

The BJP retained all six municipal corporations while the Congress wrested 23 of the 31 district panchayats and 113 of 193 taluka panchayats. The BJP continued to hold on to nagar palikas (town councils) winning 42 of the 56 municipalities, and there was only one woman who had made it happen amidst all the outrage and agitation: Anandiben. For her, not trying was worse than failing. No matter what, she stood up, risked her life and campaigned for the party. Her only mission was to serve the party and the people.

Wins in all major cities saved the BJP the embarrassment, but rural Gujarat had given an early wake-up call to the party that had never lost an election during Modi's stint as chief minister

---

[30]PTI, 'In Modi's Gujarat, Congress Sweeps Civic Polls in Rural Areas, BJP Retains Hold in Urban Pockets', *The Times of India*, 3 December 2015, https://bit.ly/3vOXhz2. Accessed on 9 August 2022.

(2001–14). This was the moment for Anandiben to take a step back and engage in retrospection. She knew the result was a direct consequence of the Patidar agitation. She could not have agreed to any of the demands and losing the elections by prioritizing honesty was her biggest moral dilemma. She would never let anything affect the party and its position in the state, yet, there were her principles to consider too.

WAKE-UP CALL FOR ANANDIBEN![31]

This was the news headline after the results were declared. The results were an indicator of the changing political tide ahead of the 2017 assembly polls and the Congress was pleased with its performance after having been out of power for almost two decades.

When the media asked for a comment, Anandiben said that the BJP had to analyse the reasons for its poor performance in the local body polls in the rural areas of the state. While addressing the party workers outside the BJP office in Kamalam, she admitted, 'Though we have done well in municipal corporations and municipalities, it is also a fact that the results in district and taluka panchayat bodies are not up to the expectations.' She stressed that although they had carried out several developmental works across Gujarat and strengthened the party organization, something had gone wrong. 'We will find out and address these problems,' she said.

After meeting the party workers post the election result, Anandiben came back home. She sat alone in her office, taking deep breaths, and gazed at the election report. Her mind was restless. She could

---

[31]'"Wake-up call" for Anandiben', *The Telegraph*, 17 September 2014, https://bit.ly/3bBOERS. Accessed on 9 August 2022.

not focus on the work, something that had never happened before. There was this strange feeling, some kind of fear that was disturbing her. That was the moment when, for the first time, the thought of leaving politics crossed her mind. She resisted the thought but it wouldn't leave her. This scenario had instilled a fear in her of losing the 2017 elections and she could not let the party suffer.

On the other hand, Hardik Patel was still in jail facing several charges. The PAAS, meanwhile, organized another month-long Ekta Yatra across 11 districts of Saurashtra, starting from Sidsar, Jamnagar, and culminating in Kagvad. The Sardar Patel Group demanded that the reservation be provided under the Economically Backward Classes (EBC) quota to avoid confrontation with the OBCs.

In its annual budget for the year 2016–17, the Gujarat government doled out over ₹5,000 crore worth of subsidies to reach out to the weaker sections of the society. The social sector commanded 47 per cent of the plan outlay covering health, education, food and housing. The biggest subsidy amounting ₹4,010 crore had been given on power consumption to farmers in the state.[32] This included electricity at a subsidized rate to farmers, free-of-cost domestic power connections to poor families, and free power supply to water works of all gram panchayats and voluntary organizations in the state.

Negotiations with the Patidars failed with the seven-member committee headed by Nitin Patel, and Vitthal Radadiya, a BJP MP, held a second round. The call for the release of Hardik Patel and

---

[32]Nair, Avinash, 'Gujarat Budget 2016-17: Anandiben Patel Govt Showers Rs 5,000 cr Subsidies on Gujarat', *The Indian Express*, 4 February 2016, https://bit.ly/3dbuM8l. Accessed on 9 August 2022.

other Patidar leaders from jail gained momentum. The Patidars started a Jail Bharo Andolan on 17 April 2016, an agitation to fill up jails to affect their release. The district administration refused permission to hold the protest and issued prohibitory orders under Section 144, but the protestors defied the order. Soon, the protests turned violent as supporters clashed with police first in Mehsana followed by Varachha and other cities. Curfew, suspension of mobile internet and deployment of the Central Reserve Police Force (CRPF) came one after the other, by now a routine in the state. One Patidar leader died by suicide in Surat.

At a core committee meeting chaired by the BJP national president, Amit Shah, a decision was reached. The government launched an ordinance to provide 10 per cent reservation in state government jobs and education institutions for the economically backward sections.

Speaking to the media later, Gujarat BJP president, Vijay Rupani, said that the ordinance would be promulgated on 1 May 2016, the foundation day of the state, and a Bill would be introduced in the state assembly later. The reservations were presented to be over and above the ₹1,000 crore Mukhyamantri Yuva Swavalamban Yojana announced by Anandiben. Rupani pointed out that the state government would defend the reservation in both high court and the Supreme Court, if required. It was evident that the party was trying its best to bring an end to the prolonged Patidar agitation.

Hardik Patel was granted bail on 16 July on the condition that he leave the state for six months and Mehsana for nine months. The state government also announced that 391 cases out of the total 438 filed against Patidar community members would be withdrawn.

For Anandiben, Gujarat was going through the most critical political situation ever. In her two years, she had seen multiple protests rising and harming the state. She, however, was firm on her decision and knew that providing reservation to any community was incorrect, legally and politically. She could never let what was right bow out in the face of blackmail and pressure as it always sets the wrong precedent. So, she went the other way, the way which only she knew about, the path that her moral compass pointed towards.

The Resignation

If patience is worth anything, it must endure till the end of time. And a living faith will last in the midst of the blackest storm.

—Mahatma Gandhi

A big decision came from the Gujarat government in the last week of July 2016 received by all as ecstatic news. For over 8.77 lakh state government employees and pensioners, Anandiben announced the implementation of the 7th Pay Commission in Gujarat. She had accepted the recommendations of the commission and announced that she would implement it in the state. She had been planning this for a long time. Being a teacher, she knew what it meant for the common man.

As per the press release from the Gujarat government, the new hike benefitted employees and pensioners of the state government, panchayats and institutions that run on grants in Gujarat. 'Employees of class-4 to class-1 will now get a hike of 14.60 per cent to

25 per cent in their salaries,' said the statement. It added, 'As the Centre is now expected to start deliberations to decide the hike in allowances, the state government will take appropriate decision about allowances as per the announcement by the Centre.'[33]

After such a big decision, things were going to change drastically again but nobody had any inkling of it. The day was 1 August 2016. Amidst the rising social tensions in the state and a looming assembly poll, Gujarat's first woman chief minister, Anandiben Patel, posted a video update on her official social media account that shocked the state and the nation.

Anandiben addressed everyone in a measured tone and a carefully crafted message that brought all her emotions to the fore. In her own words, the message stated,

> I had the opportunity to take up several responsibilities as a worker in the Bharatiya Janata Party for the last 30 years. The party gave me critical assignments in the organization as well as in the government. I consider it my good fortune. From the responsibility of the Mahila Morcha to the position of chief minister, the party leadership kept immense faith in me for which I am indebted.
>
> Under the leadership of an expert organizer, a visionary, someone who is truly committed, and a respectable person, Shri Narendra Modi, I got the opportunity to work, first in the party organization and then in the government, because of which I

[33]PTI, '7th Pay Commission: Gujarat Government to Implement 7th Pay Commission from Tomorrow', *India.com*, 31 July 2016, https://bit.ly/3Qw7N6l. Accessed on 9 August 2022.

was constantly nurtured. For the last 18 years, having worked in different important departments of the Gujarat government, I have, through several creative changes, by easy implementation of new people-oriented schemes, constantly tried to bring in transparency through honest and result-oriented efforts. In May 2014, Shri Narendrabhai and senior leaders gave me the responsibility of being the first woman chief minister of Gujarat, which I think did all the women of Gujarat proud. It is natural for comparisons to take place after the chief ministership of Shri Narendrabhai for over 12 years and I was chosen to take his place, which is as difficult as counting the stars in the sky. But I am proud of the fact that nowhere have I lagged behind in maintaining the pace in taking Gujarat forward, in the course of development charted by him.

I had joined the Bharatiya Janata Party, inspired by its ideology, its principles and discipline, and continue to abide by it. For some time now, the party has introduced a tradition of senior leaders voluntarily stepping down from responsibilities when they complete 75 years of age. It is exemplary and imitable as this is how the younger generation gets an opportunity to work.

I will also complete 75 years this November. However, the Gujarat assembly election is at the end of 2017, and the biennial Vibrant Gujarat summit is in January 2017, both of which are critical for Gujarat. So, in order to give enough time to the newly appointed chief minister, I had requested the senior leaders of the party to relieve me of this responsibility two months ago. Today, once again through this letter, I humbly request the party's senior leadership to relieve me of the chief minister's responsibility.

> I have had the opportunity to serve the dignified people of Gujarat and I have tried my level best so that the benefits of the services reach the last man. I have received immense love, affection and inspiration to constantly work for the state as my family, and for this I express my gratitude from the bottom of my heart and offer my obeisance to them.[34]

In the video message shared by Anandiben, her trembling voice and teary eyes were obvious to any attentive observer. There was a note of dissatisfaction and unhappiness in her address. The woman who had given her life to serve the people was stepping down. The woman who had thought of nothing but of her duty towards the state was bidding farewell her duties.

Her father had always said, 'Don't give up!' but he had also advised her that sometimes you have to let go of the place or people who do not respect your individuality. Anandiben retained her stand on the issues and chose to give up the chair, instead. She did not find the freedom to act and, for her, preserving her values and identity was more important than anything else. She believed that she could serve the people even without being in a position of power. Above all, the party's position in the state was visibly in danger after the results of the civic body elections. She could not let her party down while following her own path. They had to go their separate ways, so, that was it for the Gujarat Lioness. She decided to step back and rest awhile.

The lioness, though, roared one last time before leaving the

[34]'Anandiben Patel Resigns as Gujarat Chief Minister', *The Indian Express*, YouTube, 1 August 2016, https://bit.ly/3pb3Jg0. Accessed on 9 August 2022.

centre stage, and it was her loudest roar of all time. The day Anandiben resigned, she also called for an emergency meeting of the education department.

While the state was in shock, Anandiben was ready to take some crucial decisions, and this time without any fear. At the meeting, she announced, 'All female medical students will get support of 50 per cent of total fees under Mukhyamantri Yuva Swavalamban Yojana. The government will also bear balance 50 per cent fee from Kanya Kelvani Nidhi. This step would make medical education for girls free.'

Everyone looked at each other and then at Anandiben. She handed over the file to Finance Minister Nitin Patel and with folded hands said, '*Jo tamari pase samasya o chhe, to mane janavo* (If you have any issues, let me know).' She then walked out of the conference room. She did not discuss her resignation or anything related to it with anyone. There were more pending decisions that she planned to resolve before leaving the office. Many of her decisions during the last days of her term made people really happy but, at the same time, Anandiben's resignation was a heartache for them.

Anandiben shares that the thought of leaving the chief minister's position occurred for the first time after the local body election results. It was not driven by any protest or pressure. A week before resigning, Anandiben had met her children over dinner, where she had told them about her decision. '*Jo tame te kari rahya chho, toh te barabar hovu joiye* (If you are doing it, it must be right),' Anar had responded.

For other people, a resignation is a very big decision, but for Anandiben, it was the same as getting to know that she was becoming chief minister. It didn't mean that she was unemotional, just that power had no allure for her. Gaining or losing positions had never affected her personal life and her children knew that very well. They had seen her leaving the job of a principal for a greater cause and fighting against unfair practices.

Anandiben remembers the incident of leaving the Mahila Vikas Greh after an unknown person had accused her of misusing organization property. When her father had come to know about this, he had immediately asked Anandiben to leave. He knew his daughter would never do wrong but holding on to one's respect took priority over everything.

A few days before resigning from the chief minister's post, Anandiben had informed Shri Ram Lal, who was then the general secretary of the BJP in Gujarat. As the news spread to the senior leaders, she was asked what her reasons for resigning were and she had said she had three.

Amit Shah called her and asked her to send him the resignation letter before posting it. Anandiben shared the letter on his request, which was further shared with Prime Minister Modi. However, before she heard back from them or was given a 'go ahead' signal, she had posted it.

Anandiben's offer to resign, via a Facebook post, came close on the heels of a growing Dalit unrest in Gujarat and the violent Patidar agitation that had been going on since 2015. Consequently, the resignation was automatically viewed as the BJP's quick-fix response to the unprecedented crisis.

The BJP had been acing the assembly elections in Gujarat for the last 18 years, and for almost 11 years out of that, Prime

Minister Modi had been at the helm. For the BJP, Gujarat was a prestige state. The Gujarat model of economic development had been one of the most crucial factors that had helped the party secure a majority on its own in the 2014 general elections. Yet, a state of perpetual social crisis had gripped Gujarat for more than two years and there was no sign of respite.

The unfortunate fact was that the unrest had occurred under the leadership of Anandiben, who carried the distinction of being the first woman chief minister of Gujarat and who Modi had chosen to be his successor. More than the protests, it was the restrictions that Anandiben faced in decision-making while handling the protests her own way that had worsened the narrative for her.

Whatever the outcome, the fact remained that the BJP was losing its grip over the state's politics after these protests, and something needed to be done quickly. The BJP was hard-pressed to ensure it did not lose Gujarat. While Anandiben was anguished after submitting her resignation, the political climate had steadily turned against her since the agitation had broken out. The party was in a mess, and Anandiben wanted to clean it up.

The aftermath of the Patidar protest meant that the BJP stood to lose the 15 per cent vote share that came from the community. A share that had ensured the BJP's continued electoral success in the last two decades. The dismal local body election result showed that the ground beneath the BJP's feet was shifting. Ironically, the party had failed to retain the Patel support even when the apex politician of the state government was from the same community. This was a major issue that was causing a lot of trouble to Anandiben, and she felt the problem could be fixed by her stepping down.

The Patidar protest wasn't going out of fervour, in fact, it still simmers in the social landscape of the state. What came next, however, was an even bigger blow to the ideals of Anandiben. A series of corruption charges rocked the core of everything that she stood for. Of course, they were false allegations and plain enough to understand for everyone who knew her. But these were trying times for the lioness.

The BJP had thrived in Gujarat on Modi's incorruptible reputation. His *'Na khaoonga, na khaane doonga* (Neither will I eat [read pocket public money], nor will I let anyone eat),' slogan had paved the way for a mini electoral revolution across India, leading to the UPA's demolition in 2014. Although corruption allegations ate right into party standing, the BJP put on a bold front against the charges against the Chief Minister and her daughter. Within the party, there remained an undercurrent of discomfort. Anandiben knew that the allegations were not true, hence she never let that become a reason to leave. Somebody had to pay the price for everything that had happened in the last two years to protect the position of the party, and Anandiben happened to be, by her own design, that 'somebody'.

After Anandiben's resignation announcement, statements from various politicians started flooding media channels. Rupani told the media that the decision regarding Anandiben's resignation as well as her successor would be taken by the parliamentary board. Rupani did look upset though when he expressed to the media that no one had asked the chief minister to resign and that she had chosen to quit of her own accord.

The good of the larger goal over the good of a single individual seemed to be the operating principle but everyone knew in their hearts where Anandiben stood. Anandiben had braved her own community's rebellious agitation for reservation under the OBC category in government jobs and admission to educational institutions. She did that while she occupied the highest government seat in the state. That was her grit and courage. She did not fall back or compromise for anything that was not right. She did what was feasible in the given situation but the 10 per cent reservation granted by her government under the EBC category did little to appease the ruffled feathers of the community.

The national BJP president, Amit Shah, confirmed receiving Anandiben's resignation letter and repeated Rupani's statement that further decisions would be taken by the BJP parliamentary board. Meanwhile, the Opposition was having a field day. Ahmed Patel, political advisor to the Congress president, commented that the resignation decidedly indicated BJP's imminent defeat in the upcoming 2017 Vidhan Sabha elections in Gujarat.

When the BJP Parliamentary Board met in New Delhi, they accepted Anandiben's resignation and authorized Amit Shah to pick her successor. Prime Minister Modi was in attendance too and the meeting was chaired by Shah. The board appointed Union Minister Nitin Gadkari and BJP general secretary, Saroj Pandey, as the party's central observer, to hold consultations with the MLAs for electing the new leader.

Interestingly, the chief of the state unit, Rupani, virtually ruled himself out of the race of successors, saying he would like to work for the party organization. The other names in the list of potential successors to Anandiben included incumbent Health Minister Nitin

Patel, Union Minister Purshottam Rupala and Assembly Speaker Ganpat Vasava, who was a tribal leader.

In her last week as chief minister, Anandiben decided to make the most of her pending tenure. She called ACS Rathore and discussed the next decision she was going to take while the party worked to name her successor.

As people waited for another surprise announcement, Anandiben was ticking off her list of duties. She reached Valsad to inaugurate the Aamra Van (Mango Orchard) as part of the 67th Van Mahotsav. She addressed the people there and, in her characteristic style, without any drumrolls or specialized event, announced a historic decision. Anandiben declared that small private vehicles including cars were completely exempt from paying toll tax in the state. The move was announced to be formally implemented after 15 August 2016. The revelation took everyone by surprise, including the senior leadership of BJP—Rupani and Amit Shah.

Anandiben shared that the decision was long due. She knew the problems people faced due to long queues at the tolls. The thought behind her announcement was to help people who were in emergency medical situations and had to reach their destinations as fast as possible. She shared how difficult it was for pregnant women or the elderly to cross the tolls because of the long waiting time. People were ecstatic after this decision and soon, pleas poured in for Anandiben to take back her resignation. She had always been a people's leader and people knew the importance of having her around. Her decision to step down had broken many hearts. As she kept on working for the state, people started demanding that she return and take charge.

The very next day, in a surprise declaration by Nitin Gadkari, Rupani was named the next chief minister of Gujarat, as chosen by the BJP legislators to succeed Anandiben Patel. Though it was widely speculated that the mantle would fall on Nitin Patel, Rupani emerged as the choice for the top slot at the legislature party meeting. Rupani was tasked with leading the party in the assembly polls in 2017. The party also assigned Anandiben the responsibility of supporting the party with her experience and ideas for the elections.

After winning the 2014 elections massively in Gujarat, Anandiben had been Modi's first choice to lead Gujarat after his exit. Still, she had been opposed by fellow leaders soon after the Patel agitation. Anandiben faced a decision-making crisis at that time and even Modi's support could not help her keep control over the party apparatus. Her supporters say that the party did not extend much support to her when the Patel agitation started. Some even allege that it was colleagues from her own Cabinet who had plotted against her during that time. They said that the cadre and leaders preferred to take 'orders' from party president Amit Shah instead of her. Anandiben did suspect certain conspiracies behind every political trouble she had encountered. She even discussed this with Modi, but her opponents in the party were also communicating with the prime minister's office about the political flare-ups across the state. Many BJP leaders who were in line to become chief minister also supported the protest behind her back. Anandiben would meet the protestors every night. Strict action was compromised at a lower level of authority.

In light of the Una Dalit incident, it was hard for Modi to ask her to stay when she was being questioned across the nation. The

Una violence had instant repercussions in UP, where Amit Shah had to cancel his meeting with Dalits in Agra. Instead of filling up the hall with 40,000 Dalits and giving a rousing welcome to party chief Amit Shah, the party was left with fewer than a thousand Dalits in a city that had them in huge numbers. It set off a quick chain of political events.

The Patidars boycotted and disrupted an event held for the felicitation of 44 BJP MLAs of the Patidar community in Surat by Amit Shah and Rupani. Three days later, another event in Atkot village of Jasdan Taluka, where Rupani was present, and an event in Bhavnagar for the felicitation of Jitu Vaghani, the new state BJP chief, were also disrupted. The police detained many protestors from both the sites and cancelled a PAAS rally. On the other end, the ordinance for EBC reservation announced by the state government lapsed as the case went to the Supreme Court, since its interim direction to disallow any fresh admissions or recruitment under the EBC reservation was contested.

Anandiben's resignation was not a question of 'if' but 'when' in this political landscape. Once the failure of BJP's Dalit outreach programme in UP, underlined by the Agra disaster, happened, it hastened her exit.

Many leaders alleged that under her watch, Gujarat had been slipping rapidly away from the BJP's hand. The party needed to give a message to Dalits, especially those in UP, that the BJP was concerned about the growing unrest in the community. For this reason, Anandiben had to go. But that was not *her* reason to leave.

Newspapers carried stories claiming to be from top BJP sources that a decision to drop Gujarat Chief Minister Anandiben Patel had been taken earlier the previous month and that Prime Minister Modi would decide her successor. Anandiben simply laughed at such news articles on her table every morning. At the same time, a local daily carried a statement from a source close to Anandiben. It said,

> It is well known that some leaders never accepted her authority and did everything to destabilize and dislodge her. Anandiben was known for her efficiency in administration but she obviously lacked in political shrewdness and faced infighting with some party leaders. A few senior leaders in the Cabinet never liked the fact they were overlooked, and she was made the chief minister.[35]

Two months ago, when she had completed two years in office as the chief minister, an intense media speculation had started that she was going to be removed. Several names had also been floated as the possible replacement. The source added, 'Her image was demolished using the media. People from the state were sent to brief RSS leaders and the PM about her family members' so-called interference in government.'

One senior journalist even told *The Wire* that Anandiben had complained about Shah overruling many of her administrative decisions, including that of the appointment of the police commissioner. Shah had apparently been accused of controlling the state's home ministry by Anandiben.[36]

---

[35]'Anandiben Offers to Resign, Asks Party to Elect New Face', *The Hindu*, 1 August 2016, https://bit.ly/3JGwHhq. Accessed on 9 August 2022.

[36]Mahaprashasta, Ajoy Ashirwad, 'Anandiben Patel's Resignation: More at Play than Just Administrative Failures in Gujarat', *The Wire*, 4 August 2016, https://bit.ly/3dkDykk. Accessed on 9 August 2022.

A few political workers in the BJP were of the opinion that Anandiben had failed to stand firm in the face of growing internal dissensions within the state unit of the party. According to them, state party leaders like Parshottam Rupala, Rupani, Bhikhubhai Dalsaniya and Nitin Patel were well-known rivals of the outgoing chief minister. Sources in the BJP's state unit also told *The Wire* that Nitin Patel had actively lobbied with the agitating Patels to create further troubles for her.

Anandiben's supporters claimed that her last few decisions taken shortly before and after her resignation had been intended to mark her protest and defy being branded as an administrative failure. In addition to implementing the 7th Pay Commission and withdrawing toll tax, her government also cancelled a majority of the police cases against the Patels that had been registered during their agitation.

Anandiben was a political loss in Gujarat, and it could have caused even more damage to the party while the opposition gained ground. The only factor that still went in the party's favour was the lack of any credible opposition in the state. The Congress managed to secure at least 35 per cent votes in every assembly election and had been finishing a not-so-distant second, but it had still not shown any signs of revival in its lacklustre campaigns in Gujarat. The Aam Aadmi Party (AAP), which claimed to have enrolled thousands of members in Gujarat, had not shown any electoral spark, until recently, in the 2021 civic body elections.

Despite these immediate realpolitik considerations, the message of Anandiben's hurried ousting was quite ominous for not just the party, as reflected in the BJP's anxious responses, but also for Gujarat's prospects.

Anandiben was also in the midst of a controversy when she was accused of unduly favouring the business associates of her daughter, Anar Patel, in a land deal during her tenure as the revenue minister under Modi. Around 250 acres of land in the eco-sensitive Gir Lion Sanctuary had been given to her daughter's business associates at a mere ₹15 per square metre.[37]

The media reported that the land had been given by Anandiben to Anar's business partner. The land had actually been given to Harshad Mehta and Sanjay Dhana, who were based in Dubai. Sanjay Dhana faced losses in business. He knew Anar Patel and had asked her if she wanted to dilute her equity. Anar Patel had connected him to Dakshesh Patel and Amol Bhai. When Anandiben Patel became chief minister, a Congress MP went to the press and said, 'I have something against Anandiben, though her children are not involved but I want to defame them.'[38]

When they got to know about it, the family was in shock. They could not comprehend the news. Anar Patel faced a lot of questions publicly. She decided to meet the reporter in question personally in Delhi.

'Do you know how fake news can impact someone's life?' Anar kept a file on the reporter's table and said, 'I trusted you and answered your questions, but you manipulated everything,' she continued. The reporter heard her out and realized how difficult a situation Anar had been put in.

Till today, the family faces questions related to allegations that

---

[37]Ibid.

[38]Relayed by sources close to Anar Patel.

were baseless and created to defame Anandiben's clean image.

A popular Gujarati newspaper owner had asked Anandiben for land, and she had refused. He had called Anar to his office and said, 'Ask your mother to give her resignation. I will prove you are characterless. I will prove your daughter is a drug addict. Does your mother even know how to work?'

He had laughed, and Anar had listened to him even after being the daughter of the chief minister. It was her values that had not let her react to such comments. Anar did not tell Anandiben about what had transpired between the two of them. Anar shares that, for her, Anandiben's tenure as chief minister was the toughest time for the family. From day one, people were after the family to tarnish their image and make sure Anandiben resigned. The family was scared to go out and attend family gatherings, in fear of the media picking at and manipulating even the simplest of actions.

The same newspaper had escalated the land scam news in Gujarat and compared Anar to a terrorist on the front page. Today, she laughs at it, but also feels hurt about the mentality of people and how low they can stoop in politics.

Similar allegations of undue favours have been made against her son Shwetank Patel. The children have always maintained that all such charges are baseless and that they were solely made to defame the family.

A senior RSS leader of the state explained the situation from another point of view. 'Modi was too big in stature for the protests to be directed against him. After he left for Delhi, internal rivalries sprung up within the party. Now everyone wanted a share of the profits. What we were witnessing was felt even during Modi's time but he dealt with these dissensions with an iron hand. It would be wrong to blame Anandiben alone. The crisis that the state was going through was a result of Modi's complete departure from a social model of governance to a pro-business one.'[39]

Then again, how does the RSS feature in the state party dynamics? A lot—if allegations are to be believed. For instance, it was alleged that Prakash Javadekar replaced the Smriti Irani as the Union Human Resources Minister on the insistence of the RSS. Najma Heptulla and G.M. Siddeshwara were removed from Modi's central Cabinet, also on the RSS's command. Though the BJP had cited age as their reason for removal, just like in Anandiben's case, it was not true at all.[40]

For some, Anandiben's resignation reflected the Sangh Parivar's quick political reflex. It was a sign of it maturing as an electoral force, but such damage-control could, at best, be categorized as short-term. The 'solution', as offered, did not address the real economic concerns through a series of programmatic actions. Thus, the social tensions remained with possibilities of another uprising. Maybe Gujarat was experiencing Hindutva fatigue. In that case, a strong administrative presence and focused development projects were the next best course of action. The BJP had the best person in their arsenal for exactly this kind of route, but they had unfortunately lost her in all the politics.

People who were happy and had benefitted from Anandiben's commendable work in education, development and healthcare,

---

[39]Ibid.

[40]Ibid.

were really upset after her resignation. During Anandiben's tenure as chief minister, she had laid special emphasis on social welfare programmes like malnutrition of children, women's health and building of toilets to achieve the targets under PM Modi's flagship Swachh Bharat Abhiyan, earning the reputation of a kind-hearted person. A teacher-turned-politician and recipient of the president's bravery award, Anandiben Patel had proved herself a socially conscious administrator capable of making firm decisions with her interventions in improving school education and sanitation programmes. A rare side, indeed, of career politicians!

Anandiben was and would continue to be a disciplinarian, a hard taskmaster who speaks her mind and follows the right path. She is known to be tough, but has the heart of a mother, a softer side—one that had once brought her to tears after a schoolgirl recited a poem on female foeticide. In the end, she demonstrated that she was not a leader who bows down easily when it comes to making decisions. She is a warrior who fought for three decades and, when the time came, she did not give up, she just let go to make way for better things.

On many occasions, she poured her heart out and many a time she took officials to task for their failure to serve the people. Many within and outside her party considered her to be very adamant—a trait she showed during the Patel quota stir. Instead of giving in to the demands of the agitators or offering promises, she remained firm and refused to grant the community OBC status for reservation. Instead of giving 'politically correct' answers, she bluntly told the agitators in the beginning that reservation under the OBC category for Patels was simply not possible nor was it necessary.

When Anandiben talks about her last day in office, she remembers it like any other regular day, but the entire state of Gujarat was emotional. People did not want their elder sister to leave midway, but according to her, that was the best for her party and the people who were the sole purpose of her life. She continued to work for the people until the last second, before and after tendering her resignation. In her last week in office, after her resignation had been accepted, she carried out major decisions in order to leave without regret or leave behind unattended to work. She created a situation that favoured both the people and her party, and this is what her legacy is.

The clock was ticking and Anandiben was still working on the pending files on her last day. She stood up at 6.00 p.m. It was time to leave, officially end her 30-year-long journey in state politics. The staff waited outside to bid her goodbye. Anandiben left the chief minister's office with folded hands and teary eyes. She proceeded to meet Governor Beniwal and handed over her position as the one and only female chief minister of Gujarat to date.

Within a few days, she was called by the party leadership to share her experience and provides support for the coming elections. Anandiben wholeheartedly supported Amit Shah and Rupani in planning the strategy and campaigning for the 2017 elections. Despite the news of conflict between Anandiben and the party, she appeared in rallies and went door to door asking for votes. She never stepped back from her responsibilities to the party and worked while completely detached from a certain position. The party respected her experience in the state and prepared as she suggested.

The 14th Gujarat Legislative Assembly election of 2017 led to a stunning victory for the BJP, with them bagging close to 107 seats. The Patidar and Dalit protests had dented the party somewhat but before long, the people remembered the development track too. Maybe Anandiben's relentless presence during the campaigning period refreshed the inimitable days of Gatisheel Gujarat and 100-Day Target campaign. Nonetheless, people across the state turned up in great numbers to be a part of the decisive election, 68.41 per cent, according to the Election Commission.[41] The incumbent BJP obtained a simple majority with an increase in the vote share. While the Congress's vote share and the number of seats increased compared to the last election of 2012, in the end, it was the BJP that stole the show despite all the protests and crises.

Anandiben was home reading about the result when she got a call.

'Namaste,' Anandiben said.

'*Abhaar Ben! Te tamara karana thayu* (Thank you, sister, it happened because of you),' the person on the other side said.

'*Te mari pharja hati, abhar* (It was my duty, thanks),' she replied, with tears in her eyes and peace in her heart.

She was happy that the party had won the elections; it had been the only reason she had stepped down, and now it had all been worth it. Such was her commitment to her party.

[41]'Overall 68.41% Turnout in Gujarat Assembly Elections 2017', *Desh Gujarat*, 15 December 2017, https://bit.ly/3bB8lJz. Accessed on 9 August 2022.

Anandiben believes that the entire protest was a conspiracy to malign her image.

The Patidar agitation lingered on until 2018. The PAAS supported the Congress campaign in the 2017 legislative assembly election as the party agreed to their demands. Alternatively, several other Patidar leaders also aligned with the BJP. While the BJP's performance was not as great as the 2012 show, Congress increased its share but had its private member's Bill for reservation in March 2018 rejected. It was Hardik Patel who had requested the Congress to bring the private member's Bill, and, after its rejection, he staged a 19-day fast in August–September 2018.

The 103rd amendment of the Constitution, the Bill was passed granting a maximum of 10 per cent reservation to the Economically Weaker Sections (EWS) of the society. The amendment was challenged in the Supreme Court but the government of Gujarat announced the implementation on the same date.

On 12 March 2019, Hardik Patel joined the Congress, making clear the agenda of the protest, only to leave the Congress for the BJP in early 2022.

The Lady Governor

We may stumble and fall but shall rise again; it should be enough if we did not run away from the battle.

—Mahatma Gandhi

Anandiben had underlined the conclusion of her active political career with a successful campaign and a historic win for the party in Gujarat. She decided to spend time with her family hereafter, now that she had finally taken a break after so many years. However, it turned out that one could take Anandiben out of the office, but one couldn't take the sentiment of public welfare out of Anandiben.

While Anandiben was spending time with her children, she was still working for the welfare of the people in her personal capacity. She channelled her enterprise by working with the women artisans of Gujarat associated with her daughter's NGO. As a passionate and driven individual, Anandiben could never sit idle. She was a vast reservoir of experience and knowledge and still had much to contribute for the greater good.

Perhaps the universe had taken note of this fact too. Anandiben had had a long career marked by relentless and selfless hard work. The break after her resignation seemed like a well-earned rest period, though she still kept herself occupied in her own way. Nonetheless, this interlude lasted only a few months before the nation beckoned to her again to render her service.

Anandiben was someone whose experience was invaluable and unparalleled, something more and more people acknowledge even today. Her approach to managing any system, her vision for development and her ability to overcome all impediments were much needed for other states too.

One day, Anandiben was sitting with her daughter in an anganwadi, talking to the children of the anganwadi workers, when she received a call from a senior leader of the BJP. After a few seconds of providing some basic details, Anandiben disconnected the call in her characteristic calm way.

'What happened, Maa?' Anar asked.

'I don't know. They must be planning something.'

'Will you go back?' Anar asked, raising her eyebrows.

'I would never say no to the party. I will go wherever they place me. They have made me who I am today. I will not step back from serving the people of my country as long as I am alive.'

For Anar, this answer only went on to show that her mother's ideals were not just a front but an innate part of who she was. They both smiled and continued their interaction with the children. A perfect understanding between parents and children is not only based on love but also on how values and principles are bequeathed.

A week after the phone call, an announcement was made by the president of India. It was 23 January 2018, and Anandiben Patel was named the governor of Madhya Pradesh, replacing Shri Om Prakash Kohli. The news was first tweeted by the president and then slowly published across other social media platforms.

Soon, Anandiben left for Madhya Pradesh to take charge of her next innings as governor. She took her oath under Justice Hemant Gupta at Bhopal Raj Bhavan. Anandiben, the lioness of Gujarat, was back after a gap of one year and on new turf. When she stepped down as Gujarat's chief minister in 2016, people had speculated that her decision had been influenced by the Patidar and Dalit protests in Gujarat but her own truth shone through. She fearlessly took the helm again and all allegations and speculations were rendered baseless.

On 30 January 2018, Anandiben offered a tribute on Mahatma Gandhi's death anniversary. She organized an event to celebrate the values of Gandhiji and initiated a cleanliness drive. Several competitions were held in various schools of the state to make the children aware of the exemplary life Gandhi had led.

In February 2018, Anandiben went to New Delhi and met with then president, Ram Nath Kovind. She also met Prime Minister Modi during this visit. It was her first meeting with him since her resignation as the chief minister of Gujarat. Her resignation did not feature in their conversation at all. This was a defining feature of why Anandiben had such complete faith in the party and in Modi, who would never question anyone's intention. He praised and thanked her for her support in the Gujarat General Assembly elections.

'It was my duty!' Anandiben's reply was definite, like always.

During her visit, she also met former Vice President M. Venkaiah Naidu and other senior leaders of the party like Sumitra Mahajan, Sushma Swaraj, Rajnath Singh and Amit Shah.

As the governor, Anandiben's vision was to bridge the gap between the people and the system. She considered herself fortunate to have been given a chance to work for the people again and this time there would be value addition too—she would be able to know the people of Madhya Pradesh and their diverse culture. She opened the gates of the Bhopal Raj Bhavan to the common people. This was the first time that such a gesture was extended by a governor.

Outside the big walls of the Raj Bhavan, Anandiben chose to spend time with the people and learn about their problems. She participated in 508 events in more than 35 districts within a year of her appointment. She tried to create new operational processes while keeping the old values and local norms intact.

During the initial months, she closely worked with women and children, the disabled and the tribal communities. In light of her vast experience in Gujarat, she focused on development at the grassroots levels of anganwadis, and at the foundational levels of schools and universities. In the span of her first 434 days, Anandiben attended 444 events in Madhya Pradesh.

A tree plantation event was organized at Ujjain Sanskrit University in Madhya Pradesh in which 1,000 saplings were planted accompanied by the chant of Sanskrit shlokas. In June

2018, Anandiben attended the 49th Governor's Conference at the Rashtrapati Bhawan in New Delhi, her first one in the capacity of governor. Almost two months later, an additional responsibility was entrusted to her. On 15 August 2018, following the death of Balram Das Tandon, Anandiben Patel was sworn in as the governor of Chattisgarh by High Court Chief Justice Ajay Kumar Tripathi at the Raj Bhavan in Raipur. This move by the party only went on to show how unequivocally trustworthy she was in every aspect.

Anandiben has consistently demonstrated her competence in every role assigned to her. Her expertise and track record of success gives everyone confidence in her abilities. Almost all the districts of Gujarat are an example of her planning, problem-solving and decision-making skills. She knows how to get the job done and how to do it right.

The charge of another state could not dim the indomitable spirit of this fiery personality. Anandiben conducted regular visits in villages and met people in both Madhya Pradesh and Chhattisgarh. It is rare to see Anandiben's proactive approach as a governor, who also prioritized visits to local hospitals and conducted inspections.

She also arranged for training to be given in music, drama and other fields to children living inside the Raj Bhavan.

As always, her focus was on strengthening the education system with extracurricular activities, exposure visits and sports. She met approximately 4,000 children and offered them stationery items and other necessary study material in more than 100 anganwadis. To motivate students, Anandiben participated in convocation ceremonies of more than 50 universities. She also took much interest in the progress of tourism, cultural and healthcare systems.

Anandiben made inspiring speeches when she inaugurated the Vidhan Sabha sessions in Madhya Pradesh and Chhattisgarh. Her trust in the governance machinery was firm. She regularly met the chief ministers of both states to discuss the issues of the state.

On 31 October 2018, Anandiben visited Gujarat to attend the launch of the Statue of Unity. This statue of the able statesman and architect of independent India, Sardar Vallabhbhai Patel, was the tallest in the world. This was a moment of pride for her in terms of national honour. She felt that, finally, the nation had taken a step towards recognizing the invaluable contribution of the 'Iron Man'. His distinguished leadership qualities had often been a point of inspiration for Anandiben. The statue has done wonders to the tourism industry. Every year, thousands of tourists visit the colossal statue located against the backdrop of the Satpura and Vindhyachal Hills in Kevadia, Gujarat. There is also a laser and light show, and other places of interest close by that tourists like to explore.

The Madhya Pradesh Legislative Assembly elections held in 2018 led to a hung assembly. While Congress emerged as the largest party with 114 seats, the BJP's share of 109 seats did not give the former a clear majority. The Congress claimed support from other parties and independent MLAs and informed Governor Anandiben about forming the government.

On 17 December 2018, Anandiben invited senior Congress leader Kamal Nath to take oath as the chief minister. On the same day, she also administered the oath of office for Bhupesh Baghel as the chief minister of Chhattisgarh in her capacity as the governor of the state. Both the states had seen the defeat of the ruling BJP at the hands of the Congress.

Anandiben's most important work as governor was to improve the higher education sector in the states. She consistently focused on bettering the overall examination system from start to finish—from examination to gradation. She made it convenient for the students to appear for the entrance examinations. Apart from that, she worked on cultivating the production of electricity, water and other resources in the villages; she met workers from many NGOs and beneficiaries to monitor their work; she gave suggestions and also extended government support to aid vulnerable communities; and she participated in all the meetings and conferences without delay to motivate the officials and ground workers in all departments.

In one year, Anandiben's work as the governor of Madhya Pradesh marked four world records. On 16 August 2018, more than a lakh people visited the Raj Bhavan—a first in the history of independent India. The opening up of the carefully maintained colonial architectural specimen had been a good decision.

Her tenure also marked the largest book-reading programme, Padhe Bhopal, in which 233,576 people participated.[42] What was interesting was that this reading exercise was carried out at the same time in all schools in Bhopal, and everyone read for 45 minutes. This programme also saw families giving books to children and libraries being set up. Approximately six lakh students participated by reading together.

[42]'Largest Simultaneous Book Reading Programme', World Book of Record, https://bit.ly/3dkEs0c. Accessed on 9 August 2022.

There was a plantation drive with people passing saplings of plants in a relay where a record 1,111 trees were planted.[43] Finally, she had also set a record in administering oath to two chief ministers of different states in a single day.

The most praised and talked-about initiatives of Anandiben's governorship also included health sector undertakings such as the 'TB Free' state campaign, where 4,897 people from different universities, organizations and offices adopted children suffering from TB. This step ensured that 7,212 children out of 12,899 were treated successfully.[44]

She herself adopted children from different regions of Madhya Pradesh and motivated her staff members to adopt more children to support their timely treatment. She met many children suffering from the disease and spoke with the The Tuberculosis Association of India to work proactively.

In January 2019, Anandiben ideated health camps in 128 universities and offices where more than 125,000 people got their tests done.[45] She regularly organized yoga camps at different places and inaugurated open gyms. She visited hospitals to check the arrangements and equipment.

Anandiben adopted a girl's hostel in Pachmarhi, Madhya Pradesh. She spent much of her time with the young girls there. Through them, she relived her childhood days and reminded them to avail the various education reforms and benefits. She made sure that no child was deprived of food, shelter, education or technology.

---

[43] *Pratibimb,* Raj Bhavan, Uttar Pradesh.

[44] Ibid.

[45] Ibid.

Anandiben's term as the governor of Madhya Pradesh ended in July 2019 with a transfer. On 29 July 2019, Anandiben Patel became the second woman governor of Uttar Pradesh. The ceremony took place at the Lucknow Raj Bhavan and was administered by Chief Justice Govind Mathur. She moved to a new state with the same vision of development and growth for the people.

Uttar Pradesh, the largest state in the country, is rich and diverse in every sense. It was indeed an honour for Anandiben when she became its governor. She promised herself that she would help UP become an exemplary state. Her commitment was to use her experience to uplift the state.

A noteworthy event that happened during Anandiben's tenure as governor of UP was that Yogi Adityanath invited her to deliver a lecture to UP Cabinet Ministers on how the Gujarat model was created. This is a subject close to Anandiben's heart, so she explained the process in vivid detail.

Being the head chancellor of all the state universities, her first emphasis was to develop and enrich the quality of education. She started with the recruitment of proficient and experienced vice chancellors for the universities. From the very beginning, she started guiding the vice chancellors to ensure an effective system.

Anadiben's tenure as governor of UP has been an eventful one. She was often invited to attend university convocation ceremonies where she would receive gifts. She pointed out to them that she would rather get story and colouring books as gifts, which she would then be able to give to underprivileged children. She set up many libraries, too.

Another interesting incident, an initiative to be precise, by

Anandiben was inviting school students to college and university convocation ceremonies. She requested colleges to invite children from schools as guests. Her thought behind this idea was to motivate the students to work hard and achieve their goals with dedication. This move also provided these children with exposure to higher education and the courses available. She also enrolled more than 55 lakh students in the 'Padhe Janpad, Badhe Janpad' initiative to promote education in rural parts of the state. Her 'Padhe Lucknow' initiative saw the participation of 10 lakh students.[46] It was started in several districts. Anandiben had this vision for two crore children, before the pandemic impeded her plans.

Taking the vision 'Fit India' of Prime Minister Modi forward, the Raj Bhavan Khel Pratiyogita Programme was launched in 2019 to promote the importance of health and exercise in daily life. Apart from this programme, many other initiatives were started at the Raj Bhavan by Anandiben.

Her fight to eradicate tuberculosis, started in Madhya Pradesh, was strengthened through her TB Mukt UP initiative. People in UP, especially children, suffer from tuberculosis. Chances of the patient getting cured increase manifold if the infection is diagnosed at an early stage. The Governor started a campaign where children below 18 years of age were diagnosed and treated free of cost. She wanted to make the state TB free in the next five years. A number of children were adopted by the UP government under the guidance of Anandiben and treated for the disease. She personally met the children and visited the hospital where they were undergoing

[46]Ibid.

treatment. Scores of children have been successfully cured and taken care of during the first two years of her governorship. Anandiben spread the campaign's reach not just in the cities but also in all the villages.

In August 2019, Anandiben adopted a girl child infected with TB in Lucknow. The staff of Raj Bhavan mirrored her actions and adopted 21 other children suffering from the disease.[47] This was a step towards ensuring that the children receive proper medicine and nutritious food, and lead a healthy life. All the adopted children were from an area near Raj Bhavan to enable easy and regular monitoring.

The Governor said, 'Prime Minister Narendra Modi had set a target to make India TB-free by 2025 and, keeping this in mind, the Raj Bhavan had taken the lead and decided to adopt children suffering from TB.' According to Anandiben, this was neither a show nor an obligation, but rather a responsibility that every citizen had towards the nation and its development.

She also arranged for tests to be carried out to check the haemoglobin levels in young girls, and when several were found lacking, she arranged campaigns in districts to create awareness regarding the health of young girls and how they should take care of themselves.

She is concerned with the well-being of others and it shows in her relentless efforts. She believes in open communication and is often found meeting both officers and the common people.

---

[47]IANS, 'UP Governor Anandiben Patel Adopts Girl Child Suffering from TB', *India Today,* 26 August 2019, https://bit.ly/3QwaqVL. Accessed on 9 August 2022.

Authenticity and credibility are hardwired in her. She can always be counted upon to honour her commitments.

As governor, she visited 42 districts in the first two years of her term in UP to inspect government schemes and their implementation. She worked round the clock to ensure that the state was receiving all the benefits from the government. Anandiben regularly met and discussed the developments with Chief Minister Yogi Adityanath. Anandiben was a well of experience for him to rely on. Her ability to anticipate the needs of the people and comfortably respond to situations made her a dependable ally in good governance. To date, most of the schemes introduced by her are benefiting the people.

The 50th Conference of Governors held in November 2019 selected Anandiben as the chief of the Committee of Governors. At the conference, Anandiben shared her experiences and suggested reforms in the education policy. Interestingly, the President, in his address at the conference, urged governors to make conscious efforts to connect with people, and make Raj Bhavan an accessible place. Something Anandiben had been doing since her very first appointment as a governor.

Later that month, Anandiben represented India in Mauritius at the 185th Memorial Anniversary held at Port Louis of the arrival of the first batch of Girmitiya (or Jahaji) labourers from India. The Girmitiyas were indentured Indian labourers who were sent by the British Empire to Fiji, Mauritius, South Africa and the

Caribbean to work on sugar cane plantations for the benefit of European settlers.

Anandiben marked the event at Apravasi Ghat with an inspiring speech that paid homage to the men who had travelled from her country to toil in a new homeland. She termed the UNESCO heritage spot as symbolizing 'the eternal bond between India and Mauritius…a memorial to our people's relationship of blood and sweat'.[48]

While speaking at the event, Anandiben made an interesting allusion to Mahatma Gandhi's visit to Mauritius while returning to India from South Africa, and congratulated the island nation for being an example of good democracy, both in Africa and globally. She mentioned that India was proud to partner with it in all avenues. Her visit was another link in strengthening the chain of friendship between both countries. This visit was but a glimpse of her statesmanship.

The eventful month was not over yet. On 9 November 2019, the Supreme Court's historic verdict paved the way for the construction of the Ram temple in Ayodhya. This was one of the most important and most anticipated judgments in India's history that had finally put an end to a festering dispute. The decision by the constitution bench comprising five judges headed by Chief Justice Ranjan Gogoi also gave closure to Anandiben.

Anandiben acutely remembers every part of the struggle to claim the birthplace of the God to whom billions in the country pray. She has been a part of this dream since the beginning, and

[48]'Apravasi Ghat Symbolises Bond between India, Mauritius: Governor', *Hindustan Times*, 3 November 2019, https://bit.ly/3Qeaj1e. Accessed on 9 August 2022.

that day, she was the governor of the state where the Ram Mandir was going to be constructed.

In January 2020, Governor Anandiben spoke at the inauguration of the 7th Commonwealth Parliamentary Association Conference India Region at the Uttar Pradesh Legislative Assembly, sensitizing the lawmakers about their responsibilities towards people. This was an association that was composed of over 180 legislative branches across Commonwealth countries that enjoyed parliamentary democracy. Anandiben's style of functioning involved promoting a sense of connection and harmony instead of divisiveness, and in her lecture, she urged the lawmakers to maintain the values and pride of the country.

Apart from the government machinery, Anandiben also kept a close watch on the work of social organizations. She participated in all the events and meetings to ensure the systemic utilization of resources. All her efforts benefitted the state, utmost in the department of education. With Anandiben's vast experience in the sector, the state witnessed an all-time high in the quality of both higher and secondary education.

Before Anandiben's tenure as the governor, university vice chancellors in Uttar Pradesh had been selected from the limited options available in the state's biodata bank. Anandiben made the recruitment process transparent and effective to improve the overall system. She believes that the right leaders take the system in the right direction.

For the first time, the recruitment of vice chancellors was posted in newspapers and websites to invite a wide range of applications. The result was immediate.The administration received a large number of applications from well-read and experienced professionals not only from different states but even from other countries. Anandiben created a search committee to find the best people for the posts. In this way, she handed over the universities to the most eligible applicants. The state could see the change in the education system within six months of Anandiben's appointment as governor.

She made the process transparent but difficult. No one could bypass systems to be recruited. She made sure recruitment of the faculty was strictly on the basis of eligibility and entrance exams. She made sure proper interviews would be conducted and presentations would be given (all this was not done before). She also made sure that an audit of all financial statements of universities was carried out (no audits had been done before, and the multiplicity of accounts made it all the more difficult to keep track of finances). Many such additional accounts were closed to maintain transparency and to keep in line with the new education policy. There were collaborations with the PWD, and the process of resolving the pending cases with the district and high courts was prioritized (she roped in her officials to help resolve the cases). Her team also asked universities to submit quarterly reports.

The other area of priority focus, which Anandiben consistently worked on improving, was the National Assessment and Accreditation Council (NAAC) grades for the universities. It was important because the grades impacted the grants received from the central government. She noticed that only five universities out of the 29 operating in the state had a B+ grade, which deeply affected their development.

There was only one university that had an A+ grade. Anandiben shortlisted universities and worked with them closely for them to improve to an A+ grade.

Her passion for progress was evident in her meticulous planning and problem-solving capability. She started working on the minute details with the vice chancellors and made it mandatory for the universities to get the NAAC grade and improve the grading system. This helped the universities work on data and statistics to progress in the right direction. She called for reports from the vice chancellors and professors of the universities to study the developments. She held herself accountable and made sure everyone who worked with her did so too.

She would get all the vice chancellors and PWD officers face to face on call and discuss their issues. She also suggested that social service be included in the curriculum of universities, encouraging them to adopt villages and pushing them to address malnutrition issues in anganwadis. This was all done to improve NAAC grading.

Anandiben is known for not just solving the problem at hand but investigating them to the very root to eradicate it. As soon as she became governor, she worked on more than 4,500 petitions and reference cases. Most of them have already been solved with a detailed analysis and discussion to avoid repetition of the issues.

This grassroots attention was also showcased in another historic initiative by Anandiben. She instructed each one of the state's universities to adopt five villages. The state colleges were given the quota of one village each. The state education institutions were then made responsible for a proactive contribution towards the development of the adopted villages. This practice was already prevalent in Gujarat and Madhya Pradesh, her previous turfs, and had achieved satisfactory results. The announcement for UP was made during her convocation address at the Madan Mohan Malaviya University of Technology in Gorakhpur. She further added that with direction from the vice chancellors, who would work on a blueprint detailing the activities to be performed in the adopted villages, the state's rural areas can usher in a sea change.

Anandiben had been working towards making the environment clean and green since her early years in public office. She pledged to plant 22 crore trees in an event held in Kasganj.[49] In fact, within the Raj Bhavan premises, she ideated the beautiful Panchatantra Van that has come up on around 6 acres of land. The proposed layout draws from the Panchatantra theme of ancient Indian stories with different kinds of trees and plants for a nature trail. Anandiben envisioned that the thematic forest park would attract children and impart the valuable lesson of forest conservation in them.

Unfortunately, the dreadful COVID-19 pandemic arrived right after the plan and budget were finalized. India reported its first case of coronavirus disease, which originated in China, on 30 January 2020. Anandiben carefully monitored the COVID situation in the state.

[49]PTI, '"Vriksharopan Mahakumbh" Launched with Target to Plant 22 cr Saplings in UP', *Business Standard*, 9 August 2019, https://bit.ly/3SBxKTW. Accessed on 9 August 2022.

She met the chief minister and discussed an action plan to curb the pandemic. She also asked the universities to prepare reports on the pandemic and how to check the problem of shortage of oxygen.

On 24 March 2020, the nation went into lockdown as announced by Prime Minister Modi to prevent the virus from spreading. Anandiben started relief work by procuring and distributing essentials like food rations, medicines, masks and sanitizers to the underprivileged communities. She worked with several NGOs to provide relief material to different organizations and frontline corona warriors.

During the lockdown period, the entire work at Raj Bhavan was carried out on digital platforms. Anandiben attended all the webinars and meetings through audio and video conferencing. She constantly motivated the officials to courageously fight against the pandemic. She regularly discussed the COVID-19 situation, social and health issues, and plans for treatment with then President Kovind and former Vice President Naidu. She adapted seamlessly to the digital style of functioning and attended multiple conferences and convocations during the first wave of the coronavirus pandemic.

Anandiben did not stop her work in the face of the pandemic; rather, she actively got involved in maintaining peace and patience during these dark times. She focused on the continuation of the tasks related to health and education on priority. Around the world, many leaders faced the monumental task of reassuring the public and persuading them to follow through on government decisions. As the domino effect of lockdowns and social distancing started showing in several employment sectors, the global society was facing a deepening crisis that touched many lives, especially the working middle and lower classes.

Anandiben dedicatedly urged people to prioritize a work–life balance. She appealed to both employers and employees to look after family and friends, their own overall well-being, offer flexible remote-working policies, establish strong health benefits, and maintain frequent and clear channels of communication.

As the year progressed, Anandiben found herself taking on the mantle of governorship of Madhya Pradesh once again. The failing health of the sitting governor, Lalji Tandon, led the president to entrust Anandiben with the additional charge of Madhya Pradesh. On 1 July 2020, Anandiben took oath as the governor of the state for the second time. It was a simple ceremony at the Bhopal Raj Bhavan in the presence of Chief Minister Shivraj Singh Chouhan, his Cabinet colleagues Tulsi Silawat and Meena Singh, and former ministers Kamal Nath, Digvijaya Singh, among other senior leaders.

Anandiben was never one to shy away from responsibilities and the gubernatorial charge of two big states did not deter her.

When she was governor of Madhya Pradesh, Anandiben did a tour of the Raj Bhavan there. There she saw broken houses on the premises. She got more than 40 houses reconstructed and gave people the keys to the houses. The reconstruction of another 50 houses is in progress.

She had been given an additional charge when the COVID-19 situation prevalent in the country created many impediments and crisis scenarios for the first time. She faced them all head-on and fulfilled all the functions of her post religiously.

Anandiben's focus on education is unwavering and she worked tirelessly towards the National Educational Policy 2020. She was dynamic in fulfilling her work commitments around universities and their related convocations and seminars, inaugurations and national events. She also kept a close watch on the well-being of her staff in both offices, especially during festivals, which had a mellow tone due to the ongoing pandemic.

Anandiben relentlessly stressed on working together to fight the pandemic with good habits as well as maintaining determination through good values. She regularly discussed updates on the COVID-19 situation and further action plans in both states with her staff and the state government ministers.

Everyone who has worked with her in her political career and in her previous role as a teacher admires her. They all agree that Anandiben Patel is a force to reckon with—and seemingly unstoppable.

Her Governorship Anandiben Patel has become an example for the country. Leaders and countrymen alike look up to her will and passion. Her sense of accountability, hard work and commitment to the country is unparalleled and to this day remains exemplary. As per Anandiben's juniors, she still admonishes senior officers who do not perform. Coming from someone who has never shied away from hard work, it is no surprise.

Miles to Go

My life is my message.

—Mahatma Gandhi

August 2020

Hon'ble Governor Anandiben Patel, of the two biggest states of the country, sits in her office at the Lucknow Raj Bhavan. A huge painting of Mahatma Gandhi frames her background, while a black-and-white framed picture of her parents sits on her work desk. This is the only picture she has of her parents, and it finds a place of prominence in her *karmasthala*, her workplace.

Surrounded by the values of her life, she keeps working at the age of 79 with the same passion and honesty that she displayed in her 20s. Even now, as she turns 80, she is an inspiration for many women and men across the nation. She is not just a politician; she never was one, or she would have never achieved such heights.

She stands for hard work and accountability; she genuinely cares for her people and believes in serving them. After her many stints in public office as an MLA, minister of state, chief minister and now governor, she continues to work with a zeal that is unmatched. She still carefully reads all the files, conducts video conferences, and meets hundreds of people daily to share her experiences and support them in order to facilitate the establishment of a transparent and effective governance model.

The global pandemic surges on outside but it has not been able to put a dent in her steely determination. Anandiben continues to put her best foot forward to control the situation in both states.

The first wave of the novel coronavirus was a big blow to UP, and there was also the matter of returning migrant labourers from all over the country. The situation was controlled only due to the strict actions taken by Chief Minister Yogi Adityanath and the experience of Anandiben Patel.

Soon, the states of UP and Madhya Pradesh showed a 50 per cent recovery rate of the total coronavirus patients.[50] Anandiben shared her experiences of her work during the times of severe acute respiratory syndrome (SARS) or Avian flu and other epidemics. She was constantly devising plans and analysing updates to ease the troubles of her states.

Anandiben was reading the daily news when there was a slight knock at the door of her office. '*Avi jao* (Come in),' she said, her eyes still on the newspaper.

[50]Sharma, Aman, 'Uttar Pradesh, Rajasthan, Madhya Pradesh Have Over 50% Recovery Rate', *The Economic Times*, 26 May 2022, https://bit.ly/3vPYAy2. Accessed on 9 August 2020.

'Madam, we have made all the arrangements for the pujan. We will be leaving for Ayodhya on the morning of the fifth,' OSD Ashok Desai said as he entered the office with another bunch of files.

Anandiben acknowledged him with a smile and went back to her news updates.

Amid the pervading gloom of a deadly disease catching people unawares everywhere, there was one silver lining: the Ram Janmabhoomi (birthplace of Lord Ram) bhumi pujan (breaking ground) was scheduled in Ayodhya on 5 August 2020. The foundation stone laying ceremony would be a three-day affair of Vedic rituals at the site, preceding the bhumi pujan. This was the culmination of a long legal battle with the Supreme Court that had paved the way for the construction of a Ram Temple at the disputed site in Ayodhya. A closure for a nation of devotees who only wanted to see their God resurrected in his rightful place.

Anandiben looked at the itinerary for the bhumi pujan ceremony of the Ram Janmabhoomi site. The invitation card in her hands took Anandiben back to the days when she had participated in the Ram Rath Yatra. She recalled those days of pleas and struggle, of demanding a right to honour dharma. Finally, after so many years, that struggle had borne fruit, the dream was coming true.

That day when she had greeted the Ram Rath Yatra in Gujarat years ago, was still fresh in her memory. For her, those had been the days of working as a volunteer that influenced her to join the party. She had led many women of Gujarat during the yatra and now she was going to lay the foundation stone with the prime minister and other distinguished guests.

This invitation was more than an honour for her. The COVID-19 restrictions meant that the event could include only 175 guests for the ceremony, of which 135 were seers belonging to various spiritual traditions of the country. Anandiben would be one among the only five people sharing the dais at the ceremony: Prime Minister Modi, Chief Minister Yogi Adityanath, RSS chief Mohan Bhagwat and chief of the Shri Ram Janmabhoomi Teertha Kshetra Trust, Mahant Nritya Gopaldas Maharaj.

The invitation card in her hand was a snapshot as well as a milestone of her courageous journey. Not everyone survives in the world of politics. The common belief that one compromises their morals and honesty in politics is still accepted. But Anandiben Patel is one shining example of what the determined and courageous can achieve in politics. She has shown that if you honestly work for your people without thinking about power or position, nothing is impossible. Your dedication and hard work will take you where you deserve to be. It will also let your passion for service bear results and help people on the way.

Unfortunately, the first wave of the coronavirus started climbing to a peak starting in August. India reported a record high of close to two million COVID-19 cases. It was the highest number of active cases in a month the world over since the outbreak. There was a surge in deaths, too, at almost 50 per cent increase from the previous month's fatalities.[51]

Anandiben was closely monitoring the situation in UP and Madhya Pradesh. The state governments had deployed special

---

[51]TNN, 'Nearly 2mn Cases Reported in Aug, India Sets Global Covid Record', *The Times of India*, 1 September 2020, https://bit.ly/3JGz4kk. Accessed on 9 August 2022.

teams to control the situation on the ground. The stress was on strengthening containment, increasing surveillance and testing in pockets that were vulnerable. Frontline workers and officials were also prioritizing efficient clinical management of positive cases.

This posed a serious question on the progress and safety of the Ayodhya event. This was to be a trial by fire. The government, however, was quite prepared. All pandemic protocols were strictly followed during the event. From a closely curated guest list to mandatory social distancing, every minute of the day was planned with precision, keeping all precautions that had to be followed in mind. Chief Minister Yogi Adityanath himself visited Ayodhya two days before the event to take stock of all the preparations. He took a detailed briefing from the officials on the minutest points in the run-up to the big day. He made sure that sanitization work was carried out at the Hanumangarhi temple, Saryu Ghat and all other major halts.

5 August 2020

In a maroon silk saree, the Governor walked out of her room. She was escorted by her officials and security guards to the ground floor. The convoy was waiting for Anandiben to take her to the bhumi pujan of the much-hoped-for and dreamed-of Ram Mandir. As soon as she was inside her vehicle, sirens began to blare and the governor's fleet left the Raj Bhavan premises.

She reached the Ayodhya airbase, where she was greeted by

Chief Minister Yogi Adityanath. There was a presence of staff, guards and media, all following pandemic regulations. The event would be telecast by Doordarshan and was expected to garner around 200 million viewers across the globe.

In strict adherence to his itinerary, Prime Minister Modi arrived in Ayodhya dressed in a traditional attire of dhoti-kurta. He was greeted by the Chief Minister and the Governor, and together they left for the bhumi pujan site.

The dignitaries had their first halt scheduled at the Hanumangarhi temple, a shrine to Lord Hanuman. The second point of the visit was the Ram Janmabhoomi site to pray at the shrine dedicated to Ram Lalla, the infant Lord Ram. The next destination was the site of the main ceremony.

The ceremony of the much-awaited Ram Mandir in Ayodhya began amid much fanfare. The seers who arrived from Tamil Nadu brought a gold and silver brick each with 'Shri Ram' etched onto them in Tamil. The Prime Minister laid the foundation stone amid Vedic chants and conch-shell roars. He also released a commemorative postage stamp on Shree Ram Janmabhoomi Mandir after the ground breaking ceremony.

It was a very emotional moment for millions of Hindu devotees across the world. It was just one brick but it promised a new beginning, and also an end to many years of struggle for their right. Anandiben was touched to be a part of this, even if it was in whichever small way. The party leaders had marked a historic accomplishment.

The event was watched by millions around the country and abroad on television. The Prime Minister had promised a grand temple, and he had carved the path to deliver it. 'Breaking and then rising again for centuries, Ram Janmabhoomi is free from that deviation now. Those who sacrificed and struggled, their dream became a reality today,' he reiterated.[52]

Prime Minister Modi also added, 'We will have to keep everyone's sentiments in mind. We have to ensure everyone's development with the support and trust of all. I believe this grand Ram Mandir to be built in Ayodhya, like the name of Shri Ram, will reflect the rich heritage of Indian culture. I believe it will inspire the entire humanity till eternity.'

The Archaeological Survey of India (ASI) had conducted the first excavation on the site in 1976–77 under the then director general, B.B. Lal. According to former ASI director, K.K. Muhammed, who was a part of the team, there was evidence of a temple structure dating back to the twelfth century. The second ASI excavation in 2003 corroborated the earlier findings and verified them with a ground-penetrating radar survey.

Between these two surveys, the Ram Janmabhoomi movement took the shape of a political campaign in 1984. From riots to a long-drawn legal dispute and, finally, to the historic Supreme Court verdict awarding the land to a trust for building a Ram Mandir, the thread of that recent history ran through the congregation as the first bricks were consecrated.

The sequence of events that led to this moment in Anandiben's life seemed surreal to her. In her heart, she thanked the universe for having made it possible for her to be a part of it all. Then

[52]Varma, Anuja Gyan, 'PM Modi Lays Foundation Stone of Ram Mandir at Ayodhya, Says a Long Wait Has Ended', *mint,* 5 August 2020, https://bit.ly/3PiZUQU. Accessed on 9 August 2022.

again, as the supreme philosophy of Sanatana Dharma says, 'Karma done previously brings about its fruits in proper time.' Above all, Anandiben has never been someone who is propelled by the desire for fruits or results, her work is supreme for her.

In her own words, 'It is an emotional moment for the entire country, not only for Ayodhya, and that every heart was illuminated today. I am blessed to be a part of this ceremony and be at the stage. I must have done something good.' She smiled.

Anandiben returned to Lucknow Raj Bhavan late in the night. The next morning, she woke up at 4.00 a.m. and went for a walk, keeping with her daily routine. As the day progressed, she prepared for the day ahead. She sat with her newspaper while a visiting doctor checked her blood pressure and sugar. Her favourite Gujarati breakfast was then brought to her, and she partook in a hearty plate of thepla, puran poli and khichdi. She then straight away went to her office room.

Anandiben is at her desk by 7.30 a.m. every day without fail. The teacher in her always reports on time. She is never late at starting her work unless she has previously scheduled appointments or prior meetings.

Soon, OSD Desai knocked at the door with a bundle of files and started with a brief about her day.

'Madam, you have a virtual convocation at 9.30, followed by a meeting at 10.15,' he began. Anandiben listened attentively to her schedule and when Desai was done, she said, 'Check with Chunni if she is doing fine.'

Chunni, the young girl suffering from TB whom she had adopted, was always on her mind. In the middle of her many responsibilities, Anandiben never forgot to ask about her treatment progress and health updates.

'I will, madam. Just wanted to ask if you would like to rest today?' OSD Desai had asked so knowing that it had been a tiring journey the day before to Ayodhya and back, including the whole day's engagement.

Anandiben just smiled, adjusted her spectacles and untied a thread on one of the files from the bunch placed on her table.

That is Anandiben Patel: a leader, a mother and a warrior. In her journey, both personal and political, she has seen many ups and downs. She has never backed away from any struggle in her life. She has faced every challenge and overcome it.

Like a fearless lioness, she roars at her detractors, and protects her people, her vision and the sanctity of her values. Like the indomitable matriarch, surrounded by thousands of supporters, she fights for them, at times all alone, but never gives up. All her life, she has tasted success only on the basis of sheer grit and courage. Her powerful life story gives us a simple yet important message: honesty and truth make your life hard and painful but give you the real power and freedom to do what you want to.

Anandiben's life is an example for many but what stands out is her commitment to serving the people of her country. Her passion for serving India has propelled her life's journey since the very beginning—a passion which she continues to pursue today and will do so, forever.

Acknowledgements

My journey started from a small village, spending most of the time in the fields. I am proud of my parents Shri Jethabhai and Smt. Menaben, who did not just give birth to me but also encouraged me to do achieve my dreams with deep-rooted values. They inspired me to complete my education even in difficult circumstances. I could practise discipline, and cultural and moral values in my life only because I saw them in my parents. I stood against social stereotypes all my life because I witnessed Gandhi ji's influence in shaping the thought process of our family. My father would tell us stories of the freedom struggle and his active participation, which inspired all of us at home.

When I completed 7th standard, there was no facility of further education in our village. My elder sister, Saritaben, was a teacher and she took me with her to Visnagar. She was 30 when she got widowed, even after all the challenges in her life, she made sure that her children and I complete our education. She also taught us household chores. She was an amazing woman who fought all the odds and took care of our family while respecting our culture and values. My mother and elder sisters had a deep impact on my life as teachers.

I was afraid of leaving education after completing high school. I did not know what to do next. My elder brother Devchand bhai took me to Pilvai for higher studies. I cannot explain how joyful it was to live with his family and complete my studies. I was the only girl student in my college but with the consistent support and encouragement of my principal Sh. M.S. Shah I always felt equal in every sense. I am also thankful to my professors Sh. Keshubhai Patel and Sh. N.R Shah, without them I would not have been able to complete my education. I am grateful to my husband who, in many ways, supported me in completion of my MSc and MEd after marriage.

I was a teacher for more than 30 years of my life. I express my special thanks to the school principal Sh. Daulat Bhai Desai, who taught me what all we can do for the progress of girls and their education. Whatever I learnt from him helped me when I became the education minister of Gujarat. I also want to thank my fellow teachers at Mohina Ba Girls School who always supported throughout my journey. I have deep gratitude for Dharti Vikas Mandal for allowing me to understand my social responsibilities and create awareness for the same. I could do lot of community service under the banner of Dharti Vikas Mandal.

Saving the two drowning girls in Narmada River proved to be a turning point in my life. Then Gujarat BJP president, Sh. Shankersinh Vaghela and General Secretary Sh. Narendra Bhai Modi asked me to join the party. Later, because of consistent support and guidance of Sh. Narendra Bhai Modi, I became the Mahila Morcha president, BJP Gujarat state vice president, chief minister and governor of different states. With the grace of God, I always had his values, direction and motivation with me, due to which I could do my duties well.

While I had different portfolios in the Gujarat, I got unparalleled support from Modi ji. He gave me the confidence to take tough calls, make reforms and implement new ideas for the betterment of Gujarat. I can never forget his backing and encouragement to serve the nation.

While working with Gujarat Mahila Morcha, I got immense support and inspiration from Rajmata Vijayaraje Scindia and Smt. Mridula Sinha. I want to thank them both from the bottom of my heart.

I got to learn a lot from our respected party leaders—Sh. Atal Bihari Vajpayee, Sh. L.K Advani and Sh. Murli Manohar Joshi. My heart is full of gratitude for our party leaders.

I wish to thank my son Sanjay, his wife Heena, daughter Anar and her husband Jayesh for standing as the core pillars of my life. In thick and thin, defeat and win, they stood by me. In every election campaign, they were present to support me and took the responsibility of mobilizing the citizens. After elections, they never visited my office or took favours. Sanjay and Anar supported me since their childhood. I am blessed to have children like them.

I became the Cabinet Minister for Roads and Building, Revenue, Urban Development, Urban Housing, Disaster Management and Capital Projects. I did not have prior experience in these portfolios but people like Sh. J.D Desai and Sh. Keyur Sampat supported me to bring reforms at the grassroots level. I also want to thank all the party volunteers and members who worked really hard to support me in my constituencies and serve the people at their best.

The Gujarat Model is a result of reliable and regular efforts of the party members and leaders. I want to sincerely thank each one of them. In the end, I want to thank my fellow citizens who have made me who I am today. The love, respect and support from the people is the only asset of my life. Thank you!

Anandiben Patel

